HARRY THE POLIS
AYE, THAT WILL BE RIGHT

. . .

HARRY MORRIS

BLA ... G

First published 2007
by Black & White Publishing Ltd
99 Giles Street, Edinburgh, EH6 6BZ

1 3 5 7 9 10 8 6 4 2   07 08 09 10 11

ISBN 13: 978 1 84502 175 7
ISBN 10: 1 84502 175 4

A CIP catalogue record for this book is available from the British Library.

Typeset by RefineCatch Ltd, Bungay, Suffolk

• • •

*This book is dedicated to
my Marion*

'you are my rock – love you always'

• • •

Also available from Harry the Polis:

Acknowledgements
. . .

The author would like to thank Dougie Gillespie, Ian Whitelaw, Alec Carson, Tom McNulty, Jim Duffy, Anne Nelson, Alistair Dinsmore and Fraser Mitchell for their contributions.

Special thanks to Campbell Brown and all the staff at Black & White Publishing.

Lastly, I would like to wish a speedy and continued recovery to my old mate, Jimmy Clark.

Website: www.harrythepolis.com

All enquiries to book Harry as a guest speaker or stand-up storyteller, should be directed to: info@harrythepolis.com

Postal address:

P.O. Box 7031
Glasgow
G44 3YN

Harry Morris is registered with Live Literature Events

Contents

• • •

Harry's Prayer

. . .

Gie me a sense of humour, O Lord,
And allow me tae see the joke
Then fill me wi' funny anecdotes,
Fur me tae pass on tae ither folk!
And as Ah'm telling these stories
Let the evening be happy and bright
Wi' the people who bought this book
Still laughing long after that night!
So! Fed up reading aboot Gangsta's
And the people who glamorise crime?
Well sit back and relax wi' my stories
And enjoy 'Harry the Polis' this time
Cause patter is part o' oor lifestyle
So let no man ever take that away
And make the day that I stop laughing
The day when they cart me away!

'Ye just cannae beat Glesca for the real-life patter!'

Introduction

• • •

Welcome to the fifth book in the *Harry the Polis* series.

This book is filled with stories, jokes, anecdotes and tales that hopefully will make you laugh and brighten up your day.

Read this book in whatever way you want – from beginning to end or simply picking it up and flicking through it, stopping anywhere to read a story that will cheer you up.

Harry the Polis is a series of books that you'll never, ever finish reading. It is my hope that you'll read them over and over, referring back to a certain story or anecdote that brought a smile to your face, or made you chuckle out loud with laughter.

You will find as you read this book that you just can't keep some of the stories to yourself and you'll want to share them with your friends.

Well, go ahead and start their day, and your own, with a wee laugh!

Harry

Stopping Smoking Suddenly

• • •

I received a telephone call from big Donnie Henderson, my former colleague and resident nutter.

'Harry boy! Just thought I would give you a quick call to let you know that our old ex-shift inspector Kevin Murphy died yesterday. It was quite sudden.'

'What did he die of, a heart attack?' I asked him.

'Naw! It was smoking!' he replied. 'I was with him when it happened.'

'Was it cancer?' I asked in a concerned voice.

'Not at all!' he responded. 'We were sitting in the pub together having a wee dram or two, having a right good blether, when Kevin decided to go outside for a cigarette. Unfortunately, he slipped on the newly tiled smoking area floor and walloped his head off the ground – killed him stone dead!'

'So it wasn't really smoking he died from then, was it?'

'I suppose not. Anyways, I was able to summon the services of the local Jewish rabbi to attend and say a few words over him,' Donnie said, quite matter-of-fact.

'A rabbi? But Kevin is a Catholic, so surely you mean a priest?'

Too which Donnie responded very indignantly, 'Are ye bloody joking? There's no way I was going to bother a priest at that time on a Sunday night!'

Undercover Technology

• • •

It amazes me how much modern technology plays a big part in the way we police our cities and detect our criminals in today's hi-tech society.

I remember arriving at the office one time to take up my night-shift duty and being called into the sergeant's room.

'Throw on a civvy jacket, Harry, we're going for a "steak-out" right now!' he said.

I couldn't wait to phone my missus.

'What do you make of it, darling? I'm only two weeks in the job and the sergeant is taking me out for a meal!'

Easy mistake to make, I thought.

However, as I was later to find out, it was my first surveillance assignment.

No mobile phones or radios in those days, we relied on making hand signs and noise signals to alert each other of the suspect's approach.

The suspect was spotted coming into the area by the first cop, who alerted his nearest contact, by impersonating the noise of a mating chimpanzee.

Not exactly out of place in the Castlemilk area of Glasgow.

The next cop on the stakeout would hear this and signal by making a sound like an owl out on a dark night. On hearing this, the next cop in line would bark like a dog. All very technical and, dare I say, impressive stuff!

I would be the next in the line to hear this signal and therefore it would be my turn to pass on the news of the suspect's presence.

Unable to impersonate an animal noise, or whistle like an Indian in the John Wayne film *She Wore a Yellow Ribbon*, I put the forefinger of each hand up to my mouth and signalled 'HE'S COMING!' at the top of my voice.

Unfortunately, this was probably an old, well-used method I had employed, which was instantly recognisable to neds, and apparently I inadvertently alerted every bloody criminal within a three-mile radius.

Progress would be made with the arrival of the two-way radios and, even better, with the mobile phone.

So as not to alert the suspect, if he was close by, we would use the text method. In particular the T9 system.

Now the T9 system is when you've typed into your phone the beginning of the word you want to write and the system automatically puts up on to the screen the word it thinks you want to say.

Not being very technically minded in the use of mobile phones and their many qualities, by the time I had typed in my text message, informing my colleagues that I had observed the suspect in the area, he had arrived home, alerted his entire family to my presence, packed all the family belongings into cases, called a 'fast black' and were now sitting comfortably in the departure lounge of Glasgow airport, drinking a large vodka and Irn-Bru, while awaiting the call to board flight 482 that would fly them off to Benidorm, where they would begin a new life with a whole new identity.

The following are examples of my text messages with the correct words I meant to write in brackets. It's no wonder I get into trouble!

Joist (Just) spurted (spotted) the sunbed (suspect) as he was wanking (walking) with a prick (stick) in his tight (right) hand.

I think he gay (may) have groped (dropped) the pope (dope) on his day (way), while singing (bringing) the sash (stash) to his whore (door).

He is marrying (carrying) a transvestite (transistor), in his mother (other) home (hand).

Last spurted (spotted) ejaculating (evacuating) out from the sack (back) of his mouse (house) with a large shite (white) bag, wrapped (strapped) to the poof (roof) of his bra (car).

Do you pish (wish) me to shop (stop) and starch (search) gin (him) $ (?) Ever (Over).

And how they should have read as text messages:

Just spotted the suspect as he was walking with a stick in his right hand.

I think he may have dropped the dope on his way, while bringing the stash to his door.

He is carrying a transistor in his other hand.

Last spotted evacuating out from the back of his house with a large white bag strapped to the roof of his car.

Do you wish me to stop and search him? Over.

Time Fits the Crime

...

An elderly lady appeared in court on a shoplifting charge, having stolen a tin of pears from the local Safeway.

'How do you plead?' the sheriff asked her.

'Guilty, m'lord, Ah did it!' she replied.

'How many slices of fruit were in the tin?' he asked the procurator fiscal.

The fiscal shuffled some papers about, before replying, 'There were eight slices in the tin, m'lord!'

The sheriff thought for a moment, considering his verdict, then said, 'I'm taking into account your age, but feel I have to set an example of you in order to deter you from committing a similar crime again. Therefore, there were eight slices of fruit in the tin, so I'm sentencing you to eight days in prison.'

At that, her husband shouted out from the back of the court, 'She stole a tin of beans as well, m'lord!'

Order in the Court

...

True Stories from the Law Courts

ADVOCATE DEPUTE: All your replies *must* be oral, OK? What school did you attend?

YOUNG WITNESS: Oral!

The Census

. . .

My police colleague was driving his two kids to school one morning, when he was stopped in a line of traffic.

'CENSUS' said the sign, as each driver in turn was approached by a person holding a clipboard in order to note the relevant answers to their questions.

'Good morning, sir, won't keep you a moment, but we are carrying out a government census and require you to answer a few simple questions. Now, can you tell me where you are going?' the efficient young female enquired.

'I'm going to John Street School,' he replied.

'And where exactly is John Street School, sir?' she asked.

'In John Street!' my beleaguered colleague replied.

'And why are you going to John Street?' she enquired.

'Because that's where the school is!' he replied.

'And are you all going to the school in John Street?' she asked him.

At which point my colleague paused, before answering, 'Naw, hen, just the weans. I left the school years ago!'

Forget Me Not!

. . .

Two police officers' wives were on a girlie night out and, at the end of the evening, on their journey back home, they decided to take a short cut and stagger through the local cemetery.

Halfway through, both of them were bursting for a pee and, unable to hold it in any longer, they decided to relieve themselves there and then.

Afterwards, with no paper tissues available, the first wife decided to use her knickers in order to dry herself off, before discarding them, while the second wife reached her hand over a nearby gravestone and grabbed hold of a relatively new wreath to wipe herself.

Having both dried their private parts off, they continued on their homeward journey.

Next morning, in the police muster room, the respective husbands of the two wives involved were talking and one of them remarked, 'I don't know what they two were up to last night, but when she returned home from her girlie night out, she wasn't wearing any knickers!'

To which the other one commented, 'That's nothing. My missus arrived home with a card sticking out of her fanny, which read, "We'll never forget you. From all the lads at the fire station"!'

An Old Crime Rhyme

• • •

Lizzie Borden took an axe
And gave her mother forty whacks,
When she saw what she had done,
She gave her father forty-one!

Now! I would ask you: who in their right mind would attempt to take a broken pay packet home to that bitch?

Big Issue

• • •

One day whilst working with an old colleague, not exactly known for his subtlety, we were approached by a young, dirty, unkempt youth, who put his hand out to us and said, 'Sir, I haven't eaten for three days.'

To which my colleague responded, 'Go on, force yourself!' before walking off.

What is Sex? Text

• • •

Sexthis, sexis, sexa, sexgood, sexway, sexto, sexkeep, sexa, sexthick, sexbam, sexpot, sexlike, sexyou, sexbusy, sexfor, sextwenty, sexseconds, sexat, sexleast!

Now read it all again without the word sex in it.

Was I wrong?

A Bridge too Close

· · ·

One evening, during my learning probationary period, my senior colleague approached me and said in his soft South Uist accent, 'Harry, we are going to follow PC MacLeish down the road for a bit, just to make sure he makes it home safely. He's downed a few whiskies in the back office and is ready to leave for home any minute in his private car. OK?'

'Whatever you say, Donal, you're the boss!' I replied.

Several moments later, while sitting waiting in my police panda at the rear of the station, MacLeish appeared out from a back door and gave me a wave, followed by the thumbs-up, before he poured himself into the driver's seat of his car.

Closely pursuing and bringing up the rear was Donal, who got into the police van beside me.

I started up the van and slowly followed MacLeish out of the yard and along the road, at a safe distance, for about a mile, before he turned off and drove along a local, poorly illuminated back road.

'Just keep with him, Harry, but don't get too close,' said Donal. 'Just in case he looks in his rear-view mirror and we spook him.'

Mind you, I think MacLeish had enough problems trying to focus on the road ahead, never mind what was behind him.

I kept my distance, while maintaining a reasonably close contact with MacLeish, until we came to a part of the road approaching a small narrow stone bridge.

'Right, Harry,' said Donal as he squirmed about in his passenger seat, bracing himself. 'Ease right off the accelerator and slow down here and let's create some distance between us and MacLeish, because as often as not, he has a nasty habit of clipping the edge of that bloody stone bridge.'

The words were barely out of his mouth when *bang! scud! wallop!*

'I fuckin' knew it!' said Donal like a psychic. 'It never fails – even when he drives sober, he can't avoid hitting that bloody bridge. You'd think he'd frigging know it was there by now!'

I couldn't resist my moment and said, 'Do you think he wants it moved and is maybe demolishing it in instalments, to clear it out of his way and avoid future obstructions for himself?'

Donal looked at me, deep in thought, and replied, 'Do you know what, you could be bloody right there, Harry! He's daft enough.'

At that, we followed him for another few hundred metres along the road, before turning off on a different route, as he drove into the street where he lived.

Did Ye Hear That?

. . .

A wee woman called at Castlemilk police station one day to report having lost her hearing aid.

Now this wasn't your everyday NHS hearing aid – this particular aid was bought privately and had cost her over £400, due to its sharp sound and minuscule size.

It also, due to its modern design, fitted discreetly into the ear, making it scarcely visible.

Whilst noting the loss report, she informed me that she thought it had been lost over a week earlier.

This prompted me to ask her if she could be more specific about the time and date of her loss.

I had naturally assumed that she would have been listening to somebody talking one minute, then hear absolutely nothing and realise there and then that she had lost her hearing aid, but apparently, because deaf people tend to lip-read all the time, she didn't realise she wasn't hearing anything until the night before, when she'd tried to adjust it whilst watching *Coronation Street* on the television and realised she couldn't hear Ken Barlow talking, and that was because . . . she wasn't wearing it!

Never Trust a Woman

. . .

A man and woman were involved in a road accident, whereby their vehicles were totally written off but, amazingly, neither of them were injured.

After they both crawled from their cars, the woman driver said, 'Gee whiz! Would you just look at our cars – they're totally demolished, but fortunately we are both all right! You're a man and I'm a woman – this must be a sign from God that we were destined to meet as friends and live in peace and harmony for the rest of our lives.'

Flattered by this statement, the man replied, 'Absolutely! I agree with you completely!'

The woman continued, 'Look! There's another miracle – my car is completely wrecked, yet this bottle of wine did not break. Surely it's another sign that God wants us to drink it and celebrate our good fortune?'

She handed the bottle to the man who nodded his head in agreement, opened it up and drank half of it down, before handing it back to the woman.

The woman took the bottle and put the cork back in it.

'Aren't you having a drink?' asked the man.

'No,' she replied, 'I think I'll just wait for the police to arrive.'

Playtime

. . .

One of the many duties of a police cadet is to assist at certain times in and around the police station.

One particular day, the force station assistant was engaged in dealing with another matter when a member of the public attended at the station to report the theft of his motor vehicle.

The young cadet, eager to assist, decided to note the report, taking down all the details from the reporter.

Later that same day, the reporter's car was recovered abandoned and the duty officer looked out the crime report from the file, in order to contact the owner, only to discover the reporting officer (cadet) had omitted to note down his contact details.

As a result of this, the duty officer telephoned the young police cadet at home to check with him if he had a note of the owner's telephone number in his notebook.

The telephone was answered by the young cadet's mother and the duty officer, after identifying himself to her, asked if he could speak with him regarding a police matter.

To which his mother innocently responded, 'Oh, I'm sorry, Inspector, but he's outside playing.'

Now, I wonder if his daddy was pushing him on a swing?

Check out the Library

...

Donnie Henderson, my former police colleague and trusted professional funeral mourner, contacted me out of the blue, as usual, only this time he called at the house.

'Hello, Harry boy, how the fuck are you?' he greeted me in his own inimitable, subtle style, making use of a Glasgow endearment.

'I'm fine thanks, Donnie, and before you ask me, I definitely don't wish to go to another funeral with you, so let's cut to the chase. What other little scam have you devised for me this time?' I asked, expecting the worse.

'Right, are you quite finished giving me the sermon? Because you're never going to believe this one, Harry, but I was in my local library the other day and – I kid you not – they are advertising for "Support Groups for Breastfeeding Classes"! Can you imagine it? You and me supplying the necessary support needed to hold up some voluptuous pair of young "Bristol Cities", while they demonstrate breastfeeding! I just can't resist it, Harry, I'm putting my name down as a volunteer supporter and I'm taking every class, I've just got to be a part of this. "Help in the community" and all that. Oh, and by the way, ye get a discount off the course if you're on invalidity.'

At that point, he winked at me.

'You probably don't know this, Harry boy, but I'm a keen supporter of breastfeeding, having been breastfed on Marvel powder as a boy up until I was given the real thing, but by then, I had reached the age of seventeen years and was eventually put off for biting! Will I put your name down for the role of a caring and willing "supporter" of the young voluptuous Bristol Cities? We're bound to get a good laugh, and who knows, if we're lucky, maybe even an unexpected mouthful. Just think about it for a minute – if this is a success, who knows, the next course they run could be nappy-changing classes, where they require some mature adult models to help out!' he suggested, while performing a 'Nudge, nudge, know what I mean?' gesture, tapping away with his forefinger on the side of his nose.

There was silence for a few moments, while I digested what Donnie had just said to me, before I replied, 'You are one sick man, Donnie Henderson!'

'Correct!' he responded proudly, sporting a big grin. 'So what's your answer, Harry boy? Are we going for a double, one of us on each side of a young pregnant mother, assisting in the course of motherhood, or not?'

That was the final straw for me. As I escorted him to my front door and showed him out, I said, 'Bye, Donnie. And don't call me, I'll call you.' . . . Not!

You Tube!

...

It's good to know that computer technology is helping enormously to fight crime, but this story really takes the biscuit and proves that you don't have to be very clever to work a computer.

Apparently an experienced motorcyclist is facing a lengthy ban after he 'stupidly' filmed himself with a video camera fitted to his bike, travelling at 100mph, and then posted the footage of it on the YouTube website for all to see.

This is where his lack of brains and common sense come in, because he was easily identified, due to starting his video recording of himself leaving the front door of his own house.

As it was, a serving police officer just happened to be browsing on YouTube when he came across the video playing.

Now a copy of the footage is being used as evidence to prosecute the 'speeding' motorcyclist, who was just intent on showing off.

Well, my fellow motorcyclist, I only have two words to say to you: '*You tube*!'

Black Mark for Frankie!

· · ·

During my time with a folk band, we were performing in a music festival in a place called Fyvie in Scotland.

Afterwards, Frankie learned that there was a party being held in one of the festival organiser's houses and that many of the folk music 'clique' of performers would be attending.

As a band we were slightly different from the norm. We were lively, played live music without the aid of backing tracks, and didn't play mournful dirges or sing monotonous suicidal songs about the man of the house having run off with his best buddy, 'Molly', the farm sheep-dog, following a brief affair, and been caught in a compromising position with a black-faced ewe from his herd.

Anyway, not to be outdone or miss out on a free drink, Frankie had secured the address of where the party was being held.

As we ambled our way along the streets, searching out the location, we eventually found it and, pure and simple, gate-crashed the proceedings.

The funeral – sorry, the party – was in full swing, with each of the artistes present taking it in turn to perform their party piece and sing a Scottish folk song or relate an old Scottish poem full of unpronounceable and out-of-date words.

After suffering this torture, it was a straight choice between getting pissed on the free alcohol available in the house or heading to the toilet with a razor blade in your hand to complete the objective of the present artiste, by slashing one's wrists and bleeding to death. Thereby putting you immediately out of your misery much quicker and certainly more humanely.

We decided to postpone the latter and just combine both by getting pissed and deeply depressed at the same time.

After a short while, during a long pause in the music and when everyone present was engaged in the art of conversation, this well-known female soloist, suddenly, without prior warning and, for no apparent reason as to why she would want to offend us as we hardly knew her, began moaning and howling with her eyes tightly closed and her right hand up to her head with her forefinger poked in her ear.

The house owner immediately called for 'quiet' around the room as, apparently, she was not suffering from an excruciating bowel pain, but was indeed singing.

This prompted Frankie to display some subtlety and blurt out loudly, 'Fuck me! Is that no' hellish?'

'Sshhhhttt!' A man responded. 'It's called a lament.'

'Naw pal, It's called fuckin' murder! No wonder she's got her finger in her ear. Even she cannae believe the noise she's making.' Frankie replied.

Having heard his remarks, the female singer got up from her seat and left the room apparently upset, as the owner of the house approached Frankie.

'If you don't mind, keep the noise down and show some manners. Geraldine is one of our national treasures.'

'Is that right? Well the sadistic bastert responsible for digging her up, should be jailed. Ah mean, come tae fuck mate, you've got to be winding me up. That's no' singing, she sounded like she was suffering from some heavy duty labour pains and in need of a stiff dose of the epidural stuff to put her out of her misery and give us all a break!' Frankie argued.

'Look here, if you're not enjoying it, you are more than welcome to leave.' replied the householder.

Frankie looked around the room at everyone, with some looking back at him in disgust at his outburst, before he then focussed on me.

'Harry! For fuxsakes back me up here. You must have jailed some poor basterts for making less of a disturbance than what she was doing there. Come on noo, admit it?'

I just looked straight through Frankie, trying hard not to laugh, as I did not wish to be rude but, to hell with it, I couldn't hide my feelings either . . . she was absolutely shite!

Frankie continued with his ranting and by now, he had the full attention of the entire assembled party.

'Is it me? Or have you lot just had a bit more to drink? You're not serious? You can't sit there with a straight face and tell me that was good.'

Then he pointed at an elderly couple sharing a chair and started chanting, 'Liar, liar, pants on fire!' Before snapping his fingers, like the penny had dropped and he had discovered an explanation for it all.

'Ah should have guessed it. Ah know whit it is. You're all members of the 'Fyvie Deaf Mute Society' and none of you are wearing a hearing aid tonight, right!'

'That's it. You'll have to leave. Your insults are totally unacceptable.' said the irate householder.

'Well if you can think of any better ones mate, let's hear them!' replied Frankie, sarcastically.

At that, several other big teuchter characters got to their feet to lend their physical support to the householder in his quest to have Frankie ejected.

As it was, it was time for me to intervene and persuade Frankie to leave with me before the situation became ugly and they beat us up.

Which in hindsight, was probably a better option, than the thought of Geraldine returning to the party and singing an encore.

However, as I left, I couldn't resist suggesting to the remainder of the party, that if she returned to sing and placed her finger in her ear. That was their cue, to do likewise and cover up both ears, *El Pronto!*

Order in the Court
• • •
True Stories from the Law Courts

PROCURATOR FISCAL: What gear were you in at the moment of impact?
WITNESS: My Gucci sweatshirt and denim jeans!

Harry's Wig

. . .

From *The Adventures of Harry the Polis*

(*Harry's bought himself a new hairpiece and wore it for the first time to work.*)

SPOOK: Morning, Harry.

(*Harry is standing with his back to Spook and mumbles something back. Spook then turns around and has a close look at Harry's appearance.*)

SPOOK: What you got on youse head der, man?
HARRY: Nothing! I'm just combing my hair in a different way! It's a new pattern.

(*Spook has a closer look at Harry's head.*)

SPOOK: You is wearing a syrup of fig!
HARRY: It's not a wig, or whatever you want to call it. It's the latest in hairpieces!
SPOOK: Well I hates to tell ya, but it's got da big hole in it!
HARRY: Here, you, this wasn't a cheap one, you know. They weave it into your own hair to make it look natural!
SPOOK: Well, if you's asking me, you'd have been better going to da Maryhill Carpets, at least you'd get da good underlay and free fitting with dem RUGS!

Centre Stand

...

Whilst out on motorcycle patrol duty one very hot day, my senior partner, David Hall, and I had occasion to call at an office at George Square, in the city centre.

David parked his bike on the side stand, while I put mine up on the centre stand.

Once inside the office, we removed our helmets and placed them on a nearby table, along with our motorcycle keys, and while waiting for the arrival of the person we had called to see, David came across all very smug and said, 'Oh, Harry, I forgot to mention it, but on a hot day like this, the road surface gets very soft and as a result, if you park your bike on the centre stand, the least bit of vibration can cause it to topple over.'

At that moment, right on cue, we both looked out of the office window just in time to see a bus passing and, lo and behold, because I had parked my bike on its centre stand – *clatter! clatter! bang!*

It toppled over, crashing on to the road.

David immediately burst out laughing and said in his smug manner, 'Ooops! Told you!'

I gave him a look of utter disgust for not informing me sooner of the dangers of soft tar and laughing at my expense.

Just at that moment, the person he had called to interview arrived and before engaging in conversation with him, he looked over at me and said, 'I think you have something to deal with, Harry!'

At that, I lifted my helmet and keys and left them

talking, while I walked back outside – as David thought – to pick up my 'fallen' bike, but instead of picking up my motorcycle keys from the table, I had deliberately picked up David's and walked out and over to his motorbike, which I casually mounted before starting it up.

On seeing me do this, David immediately stopped talking and approached the office window where he could only watch from inside, suffering in silence, as I smiled and gave him a wave 'goodbye', before riding off on his motorcycle, leaving him to deal with mine, still lying on the road!

The Password

· · ·

My friend and computer wizard Tom McNulty was setting up my new website on my machine and asked what word I would like to use as my password to log on.

Jokingly, I suggested 'penis'.

Without the slightest hesitation, Tom typed in the password and immediately burst out laughing as the computer replied, 'Password rejected – not long enough'!

Dumb and Dumber 1

• • •

These are two short stories about two thick neds.

The first one came about when two police officers were about to leave the station on an inquiry and discovered their police car had been blocked in by a visitor's car that just happened to have been reported stolen several days earlier.

The engine was still warm and the doors were locked.

They decided to go back into the front office and make inquiries.

Inside, there was only one person waiting to be seen and he was there to make inquiries about his brother, who was in custody.

So they decided to ask him: 'Excuse me, mate, but how did you come here today?'

'In a car. I parked it outside,' he replied.

'Is it a blue Ford Escort?' they asked.

'Aye, that's it,' he answered.

'That's a stolen vehicle, isn't it?' one officer asked.

'Aye it is,' he replied.

Guess what? He was able to see his brother sooner than he thought.

In person and in the same cell!

Dumb and Dumber 2

• • •

The second story concerns a ned who walked into a clothes shop wearing a pair of tracksuit trousers that he had stolen the previous week and set off the alarm, because he had forgotten to remove the security tag.

He was promptly apprehended by the security staff and the police were notified, who immediately recognised him for being the suspect responsible for an earlier theft at another shop, which had captured him on their CCTV cameras.

Order in the Court

• • •

True Stories from the Law Courts

DISTRICT ATTORNEY: Do you recall the exact time that you examined the body?

MEDICAL EXAMINER: My autopsy began at about 8.30 p.m.

DISTRICT ATTORNEY: And Mr Denton was dead at this time?

MEDICAL EXAMINER: No! He was sitting up on the table, wondering why I was doing an autopsy on him.

Solving yer Problems

...

I heard this joke years ago and thought I'd share it.

A wee Glesca punter walked into a pub and ordered up a large whisky and a pint of heavy beer.

The barman raised a glass up to the whisky optic on the gantry and pushed on it twice, before placing it in front of the punter. He then walked over to the taps and began to pour out his beer.

After he'd done this, the wee Glesca punter picked up the large whisky from the bar and promptly swallowed it down, following it up with the beer, as the barman stood watching and waiting to be paid.

Having downed both whisky and beer, he then apologised to the barman, saying, 'I'm sorry aboot this, big man, but I've nae money oan me. Ah jist had tae have a drink tae settle mah nerves, Ah wis desperate! But, I'll clean up for ye, or run an errand, or anything else ye might need, tae make up for the price o' it?'

The barman looked at him and deliberated for a few moments before asking, 'Anything?'

'Anything, big man, you just name it!' he replied.

'Well, there's a local hardman comes into the pub every Friday and puts a bit of pressure on me tae pay him protection money! Can ye dae anythin' aboot that for me?'

'Nae problem, big man. Jist leave him tae me, Ah've done a bit o' boxing in the past, so I'll punch his lights oot fur ye! Anything else I can do for you?' he asked.

'Aye!' the barman said. 'Can ye hear all that growling, snarling and barking?'

'Aye. Whit is that?' the punter asked.

'I've got a big Rottweiler dog in the cellar and it has severe toothache, but nae bugger can get near it tae pull the tooth out. Can ye dae anythin' aboot that?'

'Nae problem, big man, jist leave it tae me!' he said. 'Noo! Is there anythin' else?'

'Aye! Last thing,' he said. 'My auld mother lives in the flat above the pub. My auld man died sixteen years ago when she was only sixty and she has never been intimate wi' a man since. Tae put it another way, she's absolutely gagging for it! Can ye dae somethin' aboot her?'

'Jist leave it tae me, big man. It's not a problem!'

A few days later, the punter was sitting in the pub, when in walked the local hardman, to collect his protection money.

The wee punter jumped up from his seat and approached him, then, confronting him in the middle of the pub, he hit him with several body punches before landing a knockout uppercut punch to his chin.

He then grabbed hold of him by the arse and neck and promptly ran him straight out through the swing doors of the pub on to the footpath outside.

Turning to the barman, he shouted, 'Right! Open the cellar door!'

At that, he quickly ran down the steps, whereby the cellar door was closed behind him.

Growling, barking and ferocious snarling was soon followed by terrible howling, yelping and very loud whimpering.

Suddenly the cellar door was thrown open and the wee

punter appeared at the top of the stairs, covered in gooey slime, blood, loose dog fur, several claw scratches and a ripped shirt, before he blurted out, 'Right, big man! Where's the auld burd wi' the toothache?'

Extreme Makeover

...

Having sustained a serious back injury whilst on duty, I was presented with the opportunity to visit the police convalescent home at Castlebrae in Auchterarder to receive some intensive physiotherapy treatment in order to assist my recovery.

Whilst there, I met some excellent characters from police forces all over the UK with similar injury problems.

Near the end of my stay, we all decided to go for a quiet, peaceful night out to a local hotel for a drink.

We all toddled along the road, with our visible limps, walking sticks and artificial limbs.

On our arrival at the hotel, we were afforded a large table at one corner of the hotel by the staff, in order to provide our party with some privacy and also separate us from their regular customers.

However, during the evening, three of the locals made the bold decision to invite themselves over to where we were seated around the table and muscle in on our company.

To avoid any unnecessary confrontation, we continued to talk amongst ourselves and tried to ignore their presence, while they listened in and felt it necessary to include the odd remark.

One of our group, went to speak with the manageress about asking them politely to move away, but was informed that the older male was regarded as the local gangster in the area and was accompanied by two of his hardmen.

However, she had arranged for us to move into a private room, once her staff had time to prepare it for us.

Unable to do anything about them in the meantime, he returned to pass the word amongst us regarding the situation, whilst our uninvited guests began chatting with the women in our company, and after several more drinks their chat became rude and sexually suggestive.

A short time later, we were informed by a staff member that our room was prepared and we could now move into it.

Unfortunately, when we made our move, our 'gate-crashing gangsters' also made their move and followed us.

It was decided by the officer organising the night out that these three neds were just looking to start some trouble and therefore it would be better for all concerned if we drank up and left the hotel to return to the convalescent home, cutting our night short and thereby preventing any unnecessary trouble.

Everyone present agreed, except for a few who made the point that they were out for a quiet drink and were not about to be intimidated into leaving early because of some uninvited intruders joining their company.

Therefore, it was decided, they were staying on.

The lame and infirm were assisted out of the premises by those of us slightly more capable (and sober!).

An hour or so later, I was awakened by banging on my bedroom door and got out of bed to open it. Standing at the door were big Leo and Jack, who brushed past me into my room, slightly panicking.

'What's up?' I asked them, genuinely concerned by their agitated behaviour.

Leo replied in his broad Irish brogue, 'Those tree bustards started winding us up and challenging us to a fight!'

He then paused and looked at Jack.

'And? Whit happened?' I asked him, desperate to know the outcome.

Jack replied, 'Well, we just battered the fuck oot the two young guys and dragged the older bastard oot on to the street, where Leo proceeded to try and jam his head through the metal railings at the front of the hotel entrance.'

Leo then looked at me, raised his eyebrows, nodded his head and shrugged it off by saying, 'He's right. Ah dud!'

'Whit are we going to do? They're bound tae call for the polis!' Jack added, deeply concerned for the predicament they now found themselves in.

I looked at them both for a moment, before shaking my head and smiling.

'There is no way for a minute they are going to call up the polis and report that they've just been handed a severe bleaching by two crippled cops from the nearby police convalescent home. They won't want anybody to know that, or their so-called hardman reputation and image around the area will be severely dented . . . Along with their heads.'

They both thought for a moment, digesting what I had just said, before Leo asked, 'What about the manageress of the hotel? She saw us setting about them. She might report us!'

'She won't report anything,' I stated confidently. 'She'll not want her licence affected in any way and it would be the same thing if it was them that battered you. She wouldn't have seen any of it!'

After a short while, I manage to convince both of them to go to bed and forget about it.

The following morning, I was detailed along with big Leo to go to the local greengrocer's and collect the fresh fruit order for the home.

Whilst walking along the main street, we met with the manageress of the hotel who, without uttering a word, simply looked over and gave us a big smile before continuing on her way.

This was a tale of three so-called local hardmen meeting their match when they gatecrashed the wrong party.

I bet they never returned to the hotel for a while; well, certainly not until their faces had taken on an *Extreme Makeover*!

With or Without Cream

· · ·

I was invited along to an Author's Society private luncheon in Edinburgh being held in a plush hotel, where they had booked a function suite.

There were several invited dignitaries and a few celebrities and, as it was, I was seated at the side of one of the long tables, alongside an ex-army colonel, who was exceptionally polite and spoke with a mouth full of marbles; but, in saying that, we both hit it off and got on very well.

After finishing off our main meal, we were then offered the choice of cheese and biscuits, or a delicious sweet dessert. The colonel and I opted for the dessert.

Moments later, we were served our sweets and a very polite and gracious lady at the opposite side of the long table, seeing that we had taken the sweet, called out to us, 'Would you like some cream up your end?'

Too which I couldn't resist replying, 'No thanks, but if it's all the same with you, I'll have some over my chocolate gateau!'

I must admit that the colonel almost choked on several of his marbles at that response. Fortunately, it went right over her head . . . The remark, not the cream!

Billy Whizz

• • •

'Billy Whizz' was a nickname the local cops afforded a young spoiled brat from a fairly comfortable, well-off family.

Like a lot of families with reasonable wealth who tend to spoil their children, such was the case with young Billy.

At the tender age of seventeen, his father, having previously arranged private driving lessons for him around his company business yard, had also sent off and organised his driving test to coincide with his birthday.

His driving test proved to be a formality for young Billy, who passed it at his first attempt and arrived home to find a sporty little Ford with a blue ribbon tied around it and the words 'Happy Birthday' emblazoned across the windscreen parked in the driveway of his family home.

Billy couldn't wait to drive out on to the road and sample his new car.

However, over the next few weeks, Billy's erratic driving was to attract the attention of many a colleague in the station and several other road users in the area.

As a result of his 'whizzing' about, which was becoming irritable to just about every other driver on the road, Billy became a regular talking point in the police station and managed to get stopped on several occasions and issued with a form to produce his relative driving documents at the police station.

He was not only attracting the attention of the local police, but also that of the traffic department, and had been stopped for speeding, careless driving and failing to comply with traffic signals on several occasions.

However, his father intervened many times and, through his business solicitors, made numerous complaints about the police with regards to allegations of harassment and victimisation.

Due to the many complaints against the police, Billy did not appear at court to answer driving charges as often as he should have.

As a result, a decision was taken by a few of the hierarchy to issue him with a police warning, a situation that angered many police officers.

On one particular occasion whilst Archie Bauld was performing the station officer duties in the police station, Billy Whizz had occasion to call and produce his driving documents, having been stopped yet again.

Archie immediately recognised him and, after listening to his derogatory comments about the officers who had stopped and issued him with the form, interrupted him in full flow and said, 'You haven't parked this car of yours out at the front of the office, have you?'

To which Billy replied sarcastically, 'No chance, mate. Your coppers would stick a parking ticket on it, so I parked around the back of your station for safety. They can't do anything to it there!'

'Well, it will definitely be safe, that's for sure,' Archie replied.

Now, this particular station that Archie worked in was amongst a row of shops on a main street and had council houses above it, with terraced patios.

Archie handed Billy back his form and told him to take a seat in the front office and he would deal with him in due course.

'Well, don't be too long, mate, 'cause I'm on my way out to pick up my girlfriend and no doubt noise up a few of your mates in the process!'

At that, Archie went through to the rear of the station and, quietly opening the back door, he slipped outside where he saw Billy's shiny new sporty car parked unattended.

He then entered the council housing staircase leading up to the terrace entrance and, looking over the railing at Billy's new motor car, Archie picked up a very large plant pot full of pretty flowers from off the tiled terrace patio.

He then leaned over the terrace railing, where he promptly dropped the pot right on to the roof of Billy's dream machine sports car parked below, and it landed with an almighty thud.

As soon as the plant pot had left his hand, Archie took to his heels and quickly ran back down the stairs and re-entered the rear of the police station.

He then went back to the front of the office where Billy was sitting, totally unaware of the summary action that Archie had just handed out to him.

After noting Billy's driving documents, Archie allowed him to leave the station.

As a parting shot, Billy said, 'You're the only decent officer I have met in here, but no doubt I'll be seeing you again sometime.'

To which Archie couldn't resist saying, 'Maybe sooner than you think, son, but goodbye for now!'

As Billy left the station, Archie ran to the rear to listen at the door for him arriving back at his parked car.

Suddenly, all that could be heard was Billy shouting and screaming like a maniac, having discovered his extensively damaged car with a colourful flower garden growing out of the sunroof!

The Boss's Wife
. . .

During his shift duty, a uniformed police officer went into a local barber's for a haircut.

Whilst the hairdresser was giving him a trim, the door of the salon opened and in walked his chief superintendent.

Quick as a flash, the hairdresser covered the uniform cop's face with a towel and immediately left him to attend to the chief.

After giving him a haircut, the barber asked if he would like some scented lotion on his hair.

'Certainly not!' the chief replied. 'My wife would think I had been to a brothel!'

At that, he got up from his seat and left the barber's.

The barber then went over, removed the towel from the cop's face and finished off his haircut.

'I don't suppose that you'll want any scented lotion on your hair, in case your wife thinks you were in a brothel?'

To which the cop replied, 'No, go ahead. Unlike his wife, *my* wife has never been in a brothel!'

Spell It?

• • •

Having performed some renovation work on my house, I had accumulated a small pile of household rubbish, in the shape of two old doors and some plasterboard Gyproc.

I was deciding how to dispose of it, when Tank, the local scrap man from the area, approached me, having heard of my plight, and immediately volunteered to take it away and dump it.

I arranged for him to call at my house just prior to leaving to take up my police duties.

Having loaded the rubbish on to the back of his pick-up truck with the assistance of his son George, he then offered to drop me off at my station.

I agreed to his kind offer and got into the front cab of his vehicle, sitting between him and George, wearing a civilian jacket to cover up my police tunic.

On the way to the station, Tank took a slight detour and called into the Corporation Cleansing Department en route to dispose of my household refuse.

As we stopped at the gatehouse entry to the yard, the gatehouse man, armed with a pen and clipboard, came out to greet us and check on the rubbish to be dumped.

After doing so, he then approached the driver's window to speak with Tank.

'That looks like building stuff ye have there, mate, so there will be a small council charge.'

At that he wrote down the make and registration of the pick-up before asking Tank, 'Whit's yer name, mate?'

'Jimmy Krankie,' Tank nonchalantly responded.

I immediately raised my eyebrows and glanced towards Tank, who was sitting impassively as the council worker wrote the name down on his clipboard.

'Address?' he then asked.

'73 Molendinar Street, Glasgow,' Tank responded.

'How dae ye spell Molendinar Street?' he asked Tank, who then looked at me and said, 'How dae ye spell Molendinar Street, Harry?'

I quickly spelt it out for him and he wrote it on to his clipboard, before asking, 'Postcode?'

'Postcode? Who the fuck knows their ain postcode?' Tank responded.

To which the council worker replied, 'Aye, ye're right enough, mate,' before adding, 'Dump it in rubbish bay fourteen.'

As we drove up to the bay, Tank and George got out and dumped the refuse.

We were driving back out of the place when the council worker, with a grin on his face, shouted over, 'See ye later, Tank, George! And you, Harry the Polis!'

I quickly realised they had all been winding me up.

Ask a Stupid Question
• • •

The duty officer at Govan was checking on a drunk and incapable male who had been detained in police custody earlier that day, prior to him taking up his duty, to see if he was now in a fit state to be released to go home.

'Hello, John, it's Inspector Cartwright the duty officer here. How are you feeling after your sleep?'

'I'm feeling fine,' he replied as he sat up in his cell.

'Can you tell me how many drinks you consumed today?' he was asked.

'One or two, Ah think,' was his estimate.

'Well, let's put it this way,' the duty officer said, 'when did you start drinking?'

John thought long and hard for several moments before replying, 'On my eighteenth birthday, when dae ye think?'

Disabled Parking
• • •

A Glesca wag parked his car in a disabled bay and as he walked off, a parking attendant called out, 'Here you! What's your disability?'

Quick as a flash he shouted back, 'Tourette's syndrome, ya bastard – now fuck off!'

What Window?

...

I can now reveal a mystery that has probably caused a lot of confusion and prompted hundreds of questions.

'Why is there a window on that wall looking on to a brick wall?'

And the answer is very simple.

Apparently, several years ago, when the police station at Garscadden in Glasgow was being erected, it was decided that during the building process, for security purposes, a uniformed officer would be detailed his night-shift duty to be spent on the site. How boring!

It was while this duty was being performed that the officer involved, who shall remain anonymous, was searching the makeshift office of the contract builder, and discovered the building plans of the new station lying in a drawer.

As he passed the hours away, looking over the drawn-up plans, being a bit of an architectural-type person, he decided for a laugh to insert the inclusion of a window on a bare wall, making sure it was to scale.

When finished, he replaced the 'altered' building plans in the drawer.

Several weeks later, he was detailed security duty at the new station and whilst looking through it, he couldn't believe it when he entered a room with a window in the middle of the wall, looking on to . . . a brick wall! Ooops!

Gimme the Job?

. . .

I was sitting reading the paper the other day and saw a great job advertisement.

The job description was: 'Mature male wanted, must have good nature, soft gentle hands, able to give gentle massage, have good patience and willing to supply lots of TLC.'

It then went on to show you a picture of this beautiful young woman, lying naked on a sunbed, beside a private swimming pool.

I immediately called the number and was asked if I could come along right away to the Holiday Inn for a one-on-one meeting.

I didn't need to be asked twice and jumped into the car and drove straight over there!

I was pleasantly surprised to see that there were no other applicants waiting.

I was met by this young attractive lady, who asked me a few questions, like was I prepared to fly.

'Fly?' I replied. 'You bet I am!'

She then handed me an airline ticket and said, 'If you hurry, you'll be able to catch the next flight down to Manchester.'

'Manchester?' I said. 'So I take it I have the job?'

She looked at me strangely, shook her head and said, 'No, not at all. It's just that Manchester is where the end of the queue is.'

The Language Barrier

• • •

Sometimes, if we know a little bit of a foreign language, we tend to exaggerate just how much of it we really know, and we also don't like to backtrack.

Such was the case with Frankie in my folk band, when we visited Moscow to perform some concerts.

As it was, Frankie had managed to obtain some tapes on the Russian language and had played them over and over to himself.

I must admit to having heard him talking to one of the other band members, and thinking to myself, 'He's really picking up the Russian language very well.'

Unbeknown to me, although he was talking in a deeper voice and sounding very 'Russsssiannn', he was actually talking, as we say in Glesca, complete and utter pish!

This was soon to come embarrassingly to light during our first Russian press conference, when asked by one of the many reporters, assembled before us, 'Does any of your band members speak Russsssiannn?'

I immediately turned to Frankie, pointed towards him and said through our interpreter, 'Frankie has been taking Russian language lessons and has managed to pick it up relatively fast.'

Several of the reporters showed a great interest in this, as Frankie smiled at them and politely nodded his head in full agreement, delighted to be the focus.

This prompted one of the reporters to immediately direct a question at Frankie, without going through our interpreter.

Surprisingly, Frankie appeared to understand his question and, nodding his head, he replied, 'Dah! Dah!'

Impressed or what? I looked at the interpreter, raised my eyebrows and smiled. Really chuffed by this!

The reporter then smiled, before he continued by rattling off another question directed at Frankie.

Frankie hesitated for a moment, before repeating his previous words of, 'Dah! Dah!'

He then went on to string several Russian words together into a fluent sentence.

The reporter looked totally confused by this reply and said something back, as a smile broke out across his face.

At which point Frankie confidently spouted off more of his Russian patter.

There were several moments of silence before the assembled reporters, one after another, sniggered and then broke out into fits of hysterical laughter.

I turned to our interpreter, who was struggling to keep a straight face in the midst of all that was going on, and asked her, 'What did he say that was so funny?'

The interpreter replied, while trying desperately to compose herself, 'Frankie just asked him if he would like to dance, and did he own a goat with diabetes?'

Cannae Even Say It

· · ·

Out with my elderly mother, we visited the local B&Q superstore on Wednesday, the old-aged pensioner's day, to purchase some garden equipment.

As we stood in the queue waiting to be served, there was an old woman in a wheelchair being pushed ahead of us and as she reached the cashier, she asked, 'Can you tell me where your clitoris is, hen?'

The young girl immediately blushed with embarrassment, but asked the elderly customer to repeat her question.

'Can you tell me where your clitoris is?'

There was an immediate reaction of sporadic giggles and sniggers of laughter among several of the elderly customers in the queue, before the home help accompanying her leaned over and explained that what her elderly client meant to say was: 'Can you tell her where your *clematis* are?'

Order in the Court

· · ·

True Stories from the Law Courts

DEFENCE SOLICITOR: Were you present when your picture was taken?

CONFUSED WITNESS: Would you repeat the question?

Lock Up a Body

• • •

Out on patrol one day with Robert Rennie, we received a call to attend a report of a man seen jumping out of a high-rise flat.

We made our way to the location expecting the worse, but to our surprise there was nothing to see in the car park or surrounding area.

Having traced the reporter, we called at her house to speak with her and she confirmed again to us what she had seen, even pointing to the exact flat where the man had jumped from.

Back down to the car park we went to have another look for our mystery jumper, but to no avail.

I therefore broadcasted a result for the call as 'no trace' and continued with my duties.

However, about two hours later, I was to receive another call for the same location, only this time it was a report of a man injured by a motor vehicle.

Assuming it was a road accident, we again attended, where we were met by a male motorist, whiter in complexion than Casper the Friendly Ghost, reporting that he had gone to his lock-up to get his car out and on opening it up, he found the body of a man strewn across the roof of his car.

When we went around to investigate the lock-up for ourselves, we discovered that the dead man was the same unidentified male seen earlier jumping from the high-rise flat.

Apparently, when he jumped out of his window, instead

of going straight down, the swirling draught between the high-rise flats caught hold of him and blew him away from the flats and over towards the car park, eventually coming to rest when he plummeted through the roof of the lock-up, landing on top of the car parked inside.

What a shock for the unsuspecting car owner and his wife, who had been expecting to go out for a drive.

However, I suspect he had a job trying to explain the unbelievable circumstances of events to his insurance company as to how his car just happened to be written off by a pedestrian while parked securely in his lock-up garage!

Order in the Court

• • •

True Stories from the Law Courts

ADVOCATE DEPUTE: Are you qualified to give urine?
WITNESS: Huh?

Who Would Have Guessed?

· · ·

I received a call to attend and assist a home help who suspected a sudden illness had befallen her aging client.

I attended and went through the usual procedure of inquiries by asking neighbours when they had last seen him and did they know of any relatives.

After performing this duty and receiving a negative result, I made the decision to force the main door.

Several attempts later, with the use of my Doc Marten boots, the door succumbed to my pressure and I entered the house, accompanied by the home help, expecting to find the worst.

After a search of the house, I could find no trace of the occupant.

Then as I looked over at the mantelpiece, I saw a letter.

The letter contained a set of house keys and a note addressed to the home help which said:

Dear Mary (home help),

Off to visit my daughter in Cornwall for a week. I've left you a set of house keys to let yourself in and check things for me. See you when I get back.

Cheers,

Jimmy

Anniversary Gifts

• • •

Like every other man on the planet, finding the ideal gift for my wife is a task in itself, never mind a silver wedding anniversary gift for putting up with her – sorry, for putting up with *me* for twenty-five years.

So there I am, passing a shop in Argyle Street in Glasgow, when I see it: pocket taser stun gun.

The fact that she was going through a keep-fit phase, which required her to attend slimmer's clubs and gyms at night, made me confident that this would be the perfect gift to protect her and make her feel safe from the threat of any possible attackers.

And it was, after all, our silver wedding anniversary.

Now this wee gadget was a 100,000-volt, pocket/purse-sized taser, the effects of which were supposed to be short-lived with absolutely no long-term adverse affect on your assailant, thereby allowing her adequate time to move far enough away to safety. It sounded too cool!

Long story cut short, I purchased the device and took it home, where I loaded it with two AAA batteries and pressed the button . . . Nothing, nada, zilch.

I was disappointed by this first attempt, but soon realised that if I pressed the button in and then pressed the taser against a metal surface at the same time, I'd get the blue arc electricity spark, darting back and forth between the prongs . . . Totally awesome!

Unfortunately, I have yet to explain to my missus, what the brown burn spot is on the front of her new microwave oven.

OK! So I was home alone with this new toy, thinking to myself, 'It can't be all that bad or powerful, having only two AAA batteries, right?'

I sat back in my recliner with my cat Jasper looking on intently (the trusting wee soul) while I read over the instructions, and thought that I really did need to try this wee gadget out on a flesh and blood moving target . . .

No I didn't!

But for a few moments, I did think about zapping Jasper (only for a fraction of a second), but I thought better of it.

He's such a sweet cat, although he did at one time piss all over my tomato plants!

However, if I was going to give this gadget to my wife to protect herself against a possible attack from a mugger, then I needed some assurance that it would work like the instructions said. Am I wrong or what?

So there I was, sitting, wearing a pair of shorts and a short-sleeved T-shirt, with my reading glasses perched delicately on the bridge of my nose, the directions in one hand and the taser in my other.

The directions said that a one-second burst would shock and disorientate any assailant.

A two-second burst would cause muscle spasms and a major loss of his, or her, body functions.

A three-second burst would purportedly make the assailant drop immediately to the ground like a sack of potatoes, rendering his body limp and totally useless.

Anything longer than a three-second burst would be just wasting the batteries.

All the while I was reading this, I was pausing every two

seconds to look at this little device, measuring about five inches long and less than three-quarters of an inch in circumference, and, might I add, very cute, and loaded with its two wee itsy-bitsy AAA batteries, thinking to myself, 'No bloody way!'

Now what happened next is almost beyond description, but I will do my best.

So, I was sitting there alone, with Jasper the piss artist looking on with his head cocked to one side, as if to say, 'Don't do it, master!', convincing myself that a teeny-weeny one-second burst from such a tiny little gadget couldn't possibly hurt you all that bad.

So I decided, 'Bugger it! I'll give myself a one-second burst, just for the heck of it.'

I touched the prongs against my naked thigh and pressed the button.

'HOLY MOTHER OF GOD WEAPONS OF MASS DESTRUCTION! F@$$!%*CK'$^NG HELL!'

I'm pretty sure that big bullying bastard Hulk Hogan burst in through my side door, picked me up in my recliner and body-slammed both of us on to the floor – over and over and over again.

I vaguely recall waking up, lying on my side in the fetal position, with tears in my eyes, my body twitching and both my nipples on fire.

As for my testicles, they were nowhere to be found, with my left arm tucked up my arse in the oddest way, like the handle of a teapot, 'short and stout', and a tingling, pins-and-needles feeling in my legs.

Jasper was standing over me meowing like I've never

heard before and licking my face, undoubtedly thinking to himself, 'I'd love to see you do that one again, you big diddy. Go on, do it again, please!'

So here is some expert advice.

If you ever feel compelled to mug yourself with a taser, then one note of caution: there is no such thing as a one-second burst when you zap yourself, for as sure as shit in a weans dirty nappy, you will *not* be able to let go of that fucking thing until it is dislodged from your hand by some violent thrashing about of your body on the floor.

A three-second burst would be considered conservative.

Son of a bitch, that hurt like hell!

A minute or so later, I can't be sure, as time was not a relevant thing for me at this point, I collected my wits about me and sat upright, while I surveyed the room.

My bent reading glasses, which I had been wearing on my face, were now perched on the mantelpiece.

My triceps, right thigh and both nipples were still twitching away by themselves.

My face felt as though it had been shot up with novocaine and then placed under a sunbed for an hour.

I am presently searching intently for my testicles and I'm prepared to offer a substantial reward for their safe return.

A description and photo of same will follow!

Time Out

· · ·

A cop's wife awoke one night to discover her husband wasn't in the bed beside her.

She quickly slipped into her dressing gown and went downstairs to find him sitting at the kitchen table, deep in thought and sipping on a cup of coffee.

He then appeared to wipe a tear from his eye.

'What's the matter, dear?' she asked. 'Why are you sitting down here alone at this time of night?'

'I'm thinking back twenty years ago, when we were dating. I was sixteen and you were fourteen. Do you remember that?' he said.

'Yes, I remember it well,' she replied.

'And do you remember how your father caught us making love in the back of his car while it was parked in your driveway and shoved a shotgun in my face and said, "You dirty wee bastard, either marry my daughter or you'll spend the next twenty years of your life in jail for underage sex"?

'Yes! I remember it as if it was yesterday. But why are you reminiscing about that now?' she asked.

Wiping a tear from his eye, he said, ''Cause I would have been released today!'

Fix yer Motor?

· · ·

Having paid an extortionate £30 for my first motor car, the infamous Morris Mini that continually displayed teething problems and was as often as not having to be repaired, I was fortunate to secure the services of my old Glesca polis mucker Jimmy Clark.

'Whit's up with it now?' he asked.

'I don't know, Jimmy. It was as though something snapped and I had no power any more,' I replied.

'OK, Harry boy, let's have a wee look. Lift the bonnet.'

At that, I lifted the bonnet of the car and Jimmy surveyed what was before him.

After a few minutes, he had diagnosed the problem.

'Got it! It's only your accelerator cable that's come loose.'

Jimmy then grabbed hold of the loose cable and fed it back through the hole where it was held and, taking a screwdriver, he began to tighten the screw in order to secure it in place.

Unfortunately one turn too many and the securing cable part snapped off.

'Not a problem!' Jimmy said. 'We'll just nip down to a scrapyard and get one off another Mini.'

Off we went in his car to the local scrappy, only to discover, being a Sunday, it was closed.

Back we went to my car, to allow Jimmy to have another look and form a second opinion.

'I was right the first time, it's not a big problem. However, with this second look, I have to concede, Harry, without the part it's fucked and so are we.'

Now let me say at this point, I did not need it to be diagnosed as fucked, because we were both travelling together to the Tulliallan Police College the following morning in it.

Plus the fact that Clarky's car required an MOT certificate and an Excise licence to make it legal to be used on a road.

So, we were doubly fucked!

As we stood on the road pondering our next move, Jimmy looked over at another Mini parked several spaces away from mine.

'Whose it that?' Jimmy asked.

'My neighbour down the stairs,' I replied, 'he works away on the oil rigs,' not for a minute anticipating what was coming next.

'Come here a minute, Dominic,' he called to his six-year-old son.

As Dominic walked over to him, Jimmy said for him to go over to the street corner and shout 'Daddy' as loud as he could, if anybody came near.

He then turned to me and said, 'Quick! You open up the bonnet and I'll take the part off of yer neighbour's motor and repair yours with it!'

I should have protested at such an illegal request, but having rapidly weighed up the alternatives, i.e. having to get an early morning train to Stirling, or even worse, a bus, I immediately rounded on my neighbour's mini and released the bonnet catch to open it, as requested.

Jimmy moved in and within moments had removed the part we required to fix my car, thereby providing us with the necessary transport to get us up to Tulliallan Police College the following morning.

It was agreed that Jimmy would call back at my house the following week on our weekend break, whereby I would have purchased the required part to repair my neighbour's car.

As a result, no harm would be done and nobody, particularly my neighbour, would be any the wiser.

Armed with the new part, Jimmy and I went downstairs to effect the repair, only to arrive at the corner of the street to discover my neighbour had returned from his working away on the rigs early and was presently bent over the engine of his Mini, trying to work out why it wasn't working, but more importantly trying to work out where the accelerator cable part had gone.

As for Jimmy and me, we did the honourable thing . . .

We both buggered off sharpish back up the stair to my house and closed the door and hid in there until he had gone away . . . on the bus!

Vroom, vroom!

Describe It for Me?

. . .

A woman walked into the police station one day with a blind person's Labrador guide dog, still wearing the straight-handled lead, harness and fluorescent yellow vest.

She then explained to the station officer that she'd found it wandering about by itself on the footpath, no apparent owner with it.

The station officer noted the details and afterwards led the dog out to the stray kennels situated in the rear yard of the station.

Later the same day, a young newly promoted sergeant received a telephone call at the police station from the owner of the guide dog, reporting it missing.

'Well, you're in luck, because a guide dog was brought to the station earlier today, apparently wandering about the footway unattended.'

'Oh, thank goodness for that, as I feared the worst for her. She's relatively young and new to the service,' the relieved caller replied.

The young sergeant responded by asking, 'Just to make sure we have the right Labrador dog, can you describe its colour for me?'

To which the caller reacted rather indignantly, 'How would I possibly know that? I'm totally blind!'

A Well-hung Surprise

• • •

We all know the horrific story regarding John Wayne Bobbit. Just the thought of it is making my eyes water. However, I have managed to uncover some new eyewitnesses and their account of the aftermath.

Apparently, Lorena Bobbit, the accused wife of the victim, after cutting off his penis, decided this was her divorce settlement and, with it still held tightly in her hand, she jumped into the family car and drove away.

After driving for several miles along the highway, holding on tightly to his severed manhood, she suddenly opened the window and threw it out the car.

Now, by pure coincidence, Georgina and Willie Hill, a family from Glasgow, just happened to be on a fly-drive holiday in Virginia, USA, driving along the highway behind another car, believed to be the accused, minding their own business, enjoying the scenery, while munching away on pickled eggs, all washed down with cans of Irn Bru they had brought with them from Scotland, when all of a sudden – *thud!*

The penis scudded off the windscreen of their rented car, almost wedging itself under the wiper.

Quick as a flash, Willie blurted out, 'Christ, Georgie! Did you see the size of that midgie's dick?'

Now the story gets better, because after Lorena Bobbit discarded her cheating husband's manhood out the window of her car, she about-turned and drove back home where she was promptly arrested by the highway patrol, and it was nothing to do with the fact that she threw 'litter' from the window of her car on to the highway.

'Right, Mrs Bobbit, where is it?' the police captain asked her.

'Where's what?' she responded, acting dumb. (She was after all a blonde!)

'The penis?' he said.

'What penis would that be?' she replied sarcastically.

'Come on, Mrs Bobbit, we know you did it, so you might as well tell us where it is,' the police captain answered, trying to reason with her.

'Oh, awright! I threw it away,' she answered.

'What?' the captain gasped in horror.

'I threw it away – gone – vanished!' she replied.

'Where did you throw it away?'

'Along the highway, about three or four miles away.'

Some hungry coyote has probably eaten it by now

'Right!' the captain said. 'You're coming with me to show me exactly where you threw it.'

At that, he took her into the police car and they drove the few miles along the highway.

Meanwhile, J. W. Bobbit was squealing like a stuck pig and bleeding profusely from the area where his genitals used to be, and was now looking more like a transsexual who has just undergone a failed sex-change operation without the anaesthetic. (Readers, my eyes are welling up as I write this part.)

However, after directing the police to the area where she had discarded her husband's penis, the police captain *organ*-ised a search party to comb the area, in order to try and find Mr Bobbit's boaby for the surgeons to try and attach back on to his five-inch stump. (I'm joking!)

Now, if it is anything like Glasgow, when we used to get calls reporting a streaker had been sighted running along Clarkston Road, we would immediately call the radio controller and ask what was the sex of the streaker.

If it was a woman, every bugger within a six-mile radius would volunteer to attend, but if they said it was a male . . .

No bugger would bother their arse with the call.

So, try and imagine what was said during this part:

They would all spread out and methodically begin their search of the area, when a call would go out.

'Here it is. I've found it!' shouts a cop, as several others come running over for a look at it.

'Crikey! It's not a bad size, is it?' an officer remarks.

'Well, put it this way, I've seen much smaller,' remarks a gay officer before clarifying his statement: 'Purely in a professional capacity, I might add!'

Then they both look over at the officer who has found it and say, 'Well, don't look at us. Pick the bloody thing up!'

'That'll be right! I'm not touching that! Frigging hell, who knows where it's been?'

'Well, it doesn't really matter now where it's been, it's where it's going that matters. Now pick it up,' the senior cop orders.

'No way! . . . Look, I think it's still moving! . . . It is, it's still moving, it's alive! You pick it up!' the cop replies.

As they all three start arguing about who should pick it

up, when a large black female officer barges them all out the road and with one swipe, she bends down and whisks it up into her hand, walks back to her patrol car, and drives off to the hospital where a team of surgeons are standing by to perform this very difficult and delicate operation of trying to reattach it.

I'll tell you this: after I heard about this drastic action taken by Mrs Lorena Bobbit, I held on to both my wife's hands in bed at night, as well as perfecting the art of sleeping with one eye open.

I also made sure I gave my wife every pay packet I earned, unopened, for several months afterwards.

However, John Wayne Bobbit's delicate, pioneering penis transplant operation was a relative success.

The only thing, in all the excitement of performing such an unusual operation, the elderly surgeon mixed up his notes and stitched the penis on back to front, and fitted him out with two perky, 32DD breast implants.

However, the biggest problem that J. W. Bobbit has now is when he actually masturbates, instead of coming . . . he goes!

Message Boy

. . .

Some of the elderly people in the Lesmahagow area really need to be advised about what is meant by community policing.

The local community cop for the area received a call from his control room about an elderly woman wishing to make a complaint.

Could he attend and see her about it personally, as she did not wish to relate the matter over a telephone?

Later that day, the officer telephoned the woman at her home and arranged a time and date to call and see her, which was amicable, but as a precautionary measure, in case he became engaged with something unexpected, he supplied her with his mobile telephone number.

The following day, when the officer had agreed to call and see her, he received a missed call on his mobile phone, with a message left.

When the officer played it, the message was from the elderly woman, which said, 'Hello, Constable Anderson. It's Mrs Gow here. Since you are coming to see me, do you think you could bring a pint of milk and two nice buns from the baker on the main street for a wee cup of tea together?'

Bad Boy, Nice Hair

. . .

At a recent book publishing event, I was talking to a manageress from a big book store and she was telling me about how, for the first time, she had been engaged in jury duty the previous week.

The accused male in the dock sat impassively throughout the entire week-long trial, displaying absolutely no emotion or remorse whatsoever for the vicious crime he had committed, or to the evidence against him, as detailed by each and every witness.

By the end of the trial, it was without doubt, in her opinion and that of every other person present in the court, that the accused was guilty as charged.

The jury were directed to the jurors' room by the presiding judge to deliberate on the evidence they had heard and subsequently decide upon their verdict.

As the jury members sat around a table, to begin their discussions regarding the evidence, one juror immediately showed her hand by stating, 'Well, I'm voting not guilty. Ah mean tae say, ye heard his solicitor – it's the boy's burfday next week and I don't think it would be fair tae lock him up during it. Ah mean, how would you like tae open yer burfday presents in a prison cell?'

This was closely followed by a second woman, who decided that she also was voting for not guilty.

In her opinion, 'He's just had his hair cut and he suits it short. I think he looks quite handsome!'

Fortunately the evidence supporting his guilt was over-whelming and he was subsequently found guilty by the jury, who were aware of their jury duties and responsibilities to the justice system, but it certainly won't harm your defence if you look handsome and sport a brand new neat haircut when appearing at court, particularly if you get jurors like the two described, who are more intent in checking out your appearance than checking out the evidence.

Suffice to say, as he was being taken down, this good-looking young man with the neat haircut couldn't resist gesticulating towards the jury by sticking two fingers up at them, as an obvious 'thank you'.

Now, I wonder if he received a nice wee 'burfday' card and a home-made cake with a file in it from his two 'groupie' jurors.

Poor wee bugger had to spend his birthday by his cell!

Johnny Cash

· · ·

Just heard from my nephew that there is a social work van comes around the housing scheme and gives out condoms for free to anybody requiring them.

Apparently they are nicknamed the 'Johnny Cash' van, because they get them for nothing and save themselves some money.

You Look Familiar

· · ·

The duty inspector at the station had not been enjoying the best of times recently. Having been knocked out of the divisional bowling tournament, later the same day he returned to his car, parked in the car park, to discover it had been broken into and several items stolen.

A few days later, whilst performing custody officer duties, he was processing a suspect who had been brought in for car theft crimes.

As he was noting the suspect's details, he suddenly felt there was something very familiar about him.

At first he thought he had arrested him before, but no.

After several moments, the penny dropped and he realised why the ned was familiar.

He was dressed in the officer's clothing, stolen from his car during the break-in.

The youth was arrested on further charges and the items of clothing taken and lodged as productions.

'How did you know the gear was stolen?' the suspect asked.

'Because we know who owns them,' the inspector replied as he entered the extra charges on his computer.

'Right, tell me who owns them then?' he asked smugly.

The inspector lifted his head up from his PC terminal and replied, 'The man deciding whether or not you get released on report or detained in custody!'

Who's Been Eating Ma Piece?

· · ·

One day on the early shift, the ten o'clock 'piecers' returned to the station to have their meal break and the compulsory game of cards.

A couple of piece tins and Tupperware® boxes were opened around the meal table.

Suddenly the air turned blue as three of the officers discovered that their 'pieces' had been interfered with.

To be exact, each roll and every sandwich had a bite out of it and every cake, bun or biscuit was half eaten!

The only 'piece-box' with its contents still intact was that of an officer who had been careful enough to lock his piece in his locker at the start of the shift. All the others had thrown their piece-box on top of their lockers, or dookits as they were referred too.

There were a lot of accusations thrown around that day but nobody owned up.

Over the following weeks and months the mysterious phantom piece biter continued to strike on the unsuspecting, who left their piece-box unattended.

It even spread occasionally to other shifts, and not even the CID could figure out who was responsible!

The shit really hit the fan one morning when the shift sergeant, Sam Bell, sat down with the lads at their mealtime for a game of cards.

On unravelling his corned beef rolls he discovered each one had a bite out of it.

Sam went berserk, and he ranted and raved. This was going too far now – going into the sergeant's room and interfering with the sergeant's piece was overstepping the mark – big time.

Everyone on the shift was dragged into the sergeant's office and accused of the 'crime of the century', but nobody would own up and admit to it.

The following day the phantom piece biter, who I can now identify as P.C. John Forbes, was passing the sergeant's office when he overheard the sergeant and the shift inspector talking.

'I'm not having my bloody piece interfered with today, I'm away out to the bakers to get a couple of mince pies!'

At that, John headed off along the street to the baker nearest to the police station, knowing that was where Sam would go.

Arriving before him, John entered through the back door – as he had done on many occasions and pulled up a chair.

By the time the sergeant walked in the front door, John had the staff well primed.

Instead of putting Sam's order into a bag, the counter assistant made the excuse that there were fresher pies in the back shop and went through with an empty bag, and informed John that he had ordered two pies.

You can guess the rest.

The unsuspecting sergeant returned to the station clutching his bag with his pies tightly in his hand.

'Nae bugger is interfering with my breakfast today.' he was heard to say, as he sat down at the meal table alongside the rest of his shift, and John Forbes.

The look on his face was priceless, as he pulled the first

pie from the baker's bag, only to discover a large bite had been taken from it.

Fortunately, before all hell broke out in the station, and the services of Derek Acorah and the *Most Haunted* team were summoned to assist, John had the good sense to produce two fresh pies just in case. He also put his hands up and admitted to being the phantom.

Having seen the funny side, they all had a good laugh, but the game was well and truly up, for the 'Phantom Piece Biter' of Cowdenbeath!

He's Not Happy

· · ·

I called at a friend's house, who was a member of the police Dog Branch.

During my visit, he asked if I would like a bowl of his homemade soup, which I readily accepted.

Whilst sipping away at my soup, Radar, his Alsatian police dog, sat on the floor opposite.

Every time I took a spoonful of my soup, Radar would growl and snarl at me.

Feeling very uneasy at this behaviour by his dog, I informed my friend, to which he responded, 'Ach, just ignore him, Harry, he's just annoyed because you're using his bowl!'

Tight Lines

· · ·

A couple went on holiday to a fishing resort up in the north of Scotland.

As it was, the husband liked to rise early and go fishing, while his wife liked to lie in bed and read.

One morning, the husband arrived back early and decided to go back to bed for a nap.

Annoyed at this change in routine by her husband, the wife got up out of bed and, although she was not familiar with the loch, she decided to take the boat out a short distance, drop the anchor and continue to read her book.

A short time later, along came the police river boat patrol and pulled up alongside her and said, 'Good morning, ma'am. What you are doing here?'

'I'm reading a book, why?' she answered.

'Because you are in a restricted fishing area,' he said.

'Well I'm sorry, but I'm not fishing – as you can see, I'm reading my book!' she replied.

'It may appear like that, ma'am, but you have all the necessary equipment on board to fish, therefore I'll have to charge you!' he responded.

'Well if you do that, I'll have to counter-charge you with sexual assault,' the woman said.

'But I haven't even touched you!' the officer replied.

'That may be true, officer, but you have all the necessary equipment on board to do it.'

The officer then paused for a moment, before saying, 'You enjoy your book, ma'am.'

Instant Replay

• • •

Relaxing in front of his television at nine o'clock on a Sunday night, watching the final of the World Darts Championship, a divisional superintendent was shocked to see a full-scale riot taking place at the venue, in his area, resulting in fights breaking out everywhere in the hall and chairs, tables, bottles and glasses being thrown about the place.

He quickly jumped up and phoned his local station and ordered the duty sergeant and everyone on his shift to make their way to the nightclub immediately and deal with this disturbance, presently ongoing.

'But I only have one officer and myself,' the sergeant said.

'Well, I want you to call up everyone from the previous shift and recall them to duty to attend, then contact the shift relieving you and instruct them to sign on duty early and attend at the office immediately to assist with this disturbance!' he ordered. 'In the meantime, I will call the control room and have them contact the neighbouring police forces to assist us with officers.'

The sergeant duly did as instructed and then made his way along with the only cop on his shift to the locus of the nightclub disturbance.

Within a very short time, he arrived at the scene, which appeared quiet, and entered the premises.

After several minutes, the sergeant reappeared with a smile on his face and drove back in his police car to the station, where several officers who had been contacted by phone had attended to assist.

The sergeant nonchalantly picked up the telephone and called the divisional superintendent at his home, and was answered immediately.

'Superintendent Brown!'

'Hello, it's Sergeant Cartwright here, sir.'

'Right, quickly update me,' the superintendent replied.

'I take it you are watching this taking place on your television, sir?' the sergeant asked.

'Yes! Why?' he replied.

To which the sergeant had great satisfaction in reporting, 'Well, what you are watching is recorded highlights from the darts final that took place earlier today in the club at thirteen hundred hours, sir.'

There was a silence for several moments, before the divisional superintendent reacted by humbly saying, 'Thank you, Sergeant, you can stand down now.'

Next

• • •

I have just heard that they are considering opening a large, brand new Next premises in the Lesmahagow area of Scotland.

This came as quite a surprise to me, as the area is largely populated by elderly residents.

However, the confusion was soon cleared up, when I later learned that this new Next premises was nothing to do with the popular trendy clothing store, but was in fact the name of a trendy new funeral parlour. 'NEXT!'

Party Songs in the Nick
...

During an Orange walk through Glasgow, several of the police officers escorting the parade had occasion to arrest a large number of their followers, who were drunk, disorderly and causing a disturbance on the footpaths as the parade passed by.

The accused were all conveyed, singing and shouting, to the local police station and subsequently locked up in cells.

Later that evening, the police station received numerous calls of complaint regarding the noise from the station, in particular, 'The Sash' and 'Derry's Walls' being sung at the top of their voices.

The duty inspector attended at one of the complainer's households, to hear exactly what the complaint was.

After listening intently to the complaint about the sectarian songs being sung, the inspector said, 'Listen here, hen, it's our police station and we'll sing whatever bloody songs we want.'

Order in the Court
...

True Stories from the Law Courts

ADVOCATE DEPUTE: Are you sexually active?
BLONDE WITNESS: No, sir, I just lie there.

Holy Water, Hic!

· · ·

I've told you before about my missus trying to get me to give up drinking whisky and how I tried in vain the Paul McKenna method where you tap the pressure points around your face until the craving goes away.

What a load of bollocks! As a result of this deliberate self-abuse I failed miserably, ending up on the kitchen floor, beaten and bruised about the head and body and, dare I say it, requiring a drink more than ever.

However, I have now discovered a new way to discreetly cover up. I pour my bottled whisky into the ice-cube tray and put it into the freezer, then I have a glass of cool fresh water with several ice cubes in it . . . Magic!

My missus is so proud of me and the amount of water I'm drinking. She says I'm so much more healthy looking.

On the downside, now that I am tee-total, so to speak, she has enrolled me in keep fit classes at the local gym!

The Effects of Stress

. . .

An officer working night shift was awakened by his wife who informed him there was a senior officer on the telephone wishing to speak with him.

The cop got up out of his bed and went to the phone and the following is an account of what took place:

'Hello, sir, how can I help you?' the cop asked.

'Hello, John, it's about your new posting,' the senior officer said.

'Excuse me, sir, but I'm not John, I'm James,' the cop replied.

'Who?' the senior officer asked.

'James – James Smith. You know, the bar officer on the night shift.'

'Oh right. Well, what can I do for you, James?'

'Well, you phoned me, sir. I think you are looking for John,' the cop responded.

'Correct, James! Let me speak to John then,' he said.

'But John doesn't live here, sir. You'll have to phone him at his house.'

'Quite right, James, quite right. Well, if you see John, ask him to call me please,' said the senior officer.

'I'll do that, sir,' replied the confused cop.

There was silence for a moment, before the senior officer said, 'Good! Well, thanks, John . . . er, James, goodbye!'

The confused cop shook his head, replaced the receiver and returned to his bed.

'Methinks this is one senior officer having a senior moment and in need of some urgent sick leave!'

The Raid

· · ·

Big Bob was a young, six-feet four-inch cop who was built like a brick shithouse and, was about to be given his first chance at working undercover plain-clothes duties.

After only a few days of performing these duties, he was called into the drug squad office and informed he was being included on a drugs raid, at a known suspect's house.

However, intelligence reports suggested that the suspect kept a large and rather fierce looking Rottweiler guard dog in his house as an added deterrent against unexpected visitors. Therefore, it was decided that, since Bob was the biggest and newest member of the team, he should be assigned to deal with the big dog.

The team leader handed Bob a large fire extinguisher and instructed him to use it immediately on the dog should it attack them when they entered.

The idea was that, as you sprayed the frozen CO_2 at the animal's face, the cold experience of it, coupled with the noise of the liquid spraying out, would immediately nullify the dog's attack.

They left to go on the raid with Bob armed with his large fire extinguisher, which he carried around on his shoulder.

As they arrived at the door of the suspect they began the raid by smashing the door hinges, causing the door to give way.

Suddenly, from a room in the house appeared the large Rottweiler guard dog, snarling and growling fiercely at the unexpected intruders.

As it made its attack on them, big Bob stepped forward (as previously planned), with his trusty fire extinguisher at the ready. In the heat of the moment and the rush of adrenalin, Bob forgot his instructions on how to deal with the aggressive dog and promptly blootered it over the head (not as previously planned).

As a result he burst open the top of the dog's skull, as well as knocking it clean out.

This unexpected action by Bob stopped the suspect in his tracks as he tried to make his escape out of the back of the house, and he immediately returned to tend 'Bronson', who was unconscious and bleeding from the head wound!

Maybe Bob would have understood his instructions better if he had been told to 'skoosh' the dog with the fire extinguisher, then I could have added at the end of this story: No animals were injured during this raid, or at the time of writing about it!

Doesn't Compute
. . .

I decided to buy myself a computer and chose a Dell, having heard so much about them being the best, but you can't just go into PC World and purchase one, you have to book it online. So you bring up the Dell internet site and just order it . . . Simple!

The only problem is, you need to have a PC to go online to order your Dell PC and the reason I'm ordering a PC in the first place is because I don't have one!

That'll Be Me!

• • •

Two of my former colleagues were working alongside the Customs officers at Stranraer, as the lorries, coming over from Northern Ireland, were being driven off the ferry.

Their job entailed checking that the vehicles coming off were roadworthy, with valid documents, and the respective drivers were in possession of proof of identification.

During one such check, my colleague noticed that the driver was accompanied in his cab.

'Who's the passenger in your vehicle?' he asked.

Before the driver could answer him, the passenger stuck his head out of the lorry window and replied in his broad Irish brogue, 'For sure, sir! That would be me!'

Everyone a Winner

• • •

An elderly male called into the station one night with his pet greyhound on a lead.

During the proceeding conversation, the young officer, knowing the traditional occupation of greyhounds, casually slipped in the obvious question:

'Do you ever race your dog?'

The elderly male thought for a moment, before responding with a straight face, 'Not at my age, son. It would easily beat me.'

Space Oddity

...

There was panic in the crime management office at divisional HQ, with regards to the increasing rise in the number of recorded vandalisms.

Due to this increase, the crime manager, who was definitely not wishing to receive another slap on the wrist from the divisional commander, was intent on writing off as many vandalisms as possible as 'non-criminal acts'.

Such was the recent case where a half-brick was thrown through a window, which was approximately ten metres from the ground and five metres from the road, and beyond a two-metre-high wrought-iron fence.

This prompted the crime manager to immediately enquire whether or not this act was deliberate, or could the brick have been thrown up by some passing vehicular traffic.

Inquiries are now with the Chinese Embassy, NASA and the European Space Agency to establish if in fact the premises in question just happen to be in the flight path of David Bowie, Ground Control to Major Tom, etc.

If the inquiries prove negative, then the crime manager will allow for consideration to be given to the fact that it just might be attributable to a criminal act after all!

Golf Practice is Murder

· · ·

Every now and again, a court case comes up and makes a total mockery of the entire legal system and insults our intelligence . . .

Such was the murder trial involving two cousins who, to save the court time and the inconvenience to the police and civilian witnesses, had their QC negotiate a deal with the advocate depute to plead guilty to a lesser charge of culpable homicide.

Now the circumstances surrounding the alleged murder of the deceased male were thus (I submit a brief scenario as close to the actual events as possible):

Apparently one of the accused lived upstairs from the deceased, Mr Miller, and the second accused, who had only recently been released from prison on licence for a previous conviction for murder, moved into the area to share the house with him.

It wasn't long before they began to display their unsociable behaviour and total disregard for their neighbours, playing loud music and throwing numerous late-night drinking parties.

On the day of the crime, one of the youths was going out when the victim took the opportunity to go out and speak openly with him about the possibility of toning down the loud music late at night, due to his wife having just returned home from hospital after giving birth to a baby.

The accused stood with his legs apart, callously listening to what was being asked of him, while deliberately displaying utter contempt for his complainer as he looked his victim up and down.

When the talking finished, the accused then walked off without saying anything.

During the court summing up by the advocate depute, who described briefly for the judge a short summary of the events leading to the death of the victim as supplied to him in the police reports, events were described as something like this:

'Having had occasion to speak with the accused earlier that day with regard to his complaint, the victim, James Miller, a loving husband and father of a newborn baby, was leaving his house, when he was confronted by both accused outside the tenement close mouth where he resided and whereby he was subjected to a totally unprovoked and vicious attack, resulting in his death. Firstly, the accused instigated a heated argument with him, whereby they verbally abused his wife and newborn baby. During which time, one of the accused walked behind the victim, out of his view, while the other stood at his front, facing up to him and continuing with his abusive insults. Suddenly, for no apparent reason, the accused standing behind James Miller pushed the defenceless victim forward, resulting in the first accused producing a large knife from inside his jacket pocket and stabbing the victim several times in the stomach. While this was taking place at the front of the victim, the second accused, standing directly behind the victim, struck out at him with a golf club, which he had concealed on his person under his coat. He struck out at the victim so hard and viciously that the blow to his head smashed his skull. As a result of this cowardly attack, using the golf club as a weapon, parts of the victim's skull were imbedded deeply into his brain. Medical evidence was conclusive in that, if the attack with the knife, resulting in numerous, deep stab wounds to his stomach, coupled with the smashed skull, hadn't achieved the desired effect of killing him, James Miller would most definitely have sustained severe and irreparable brain damage. This was a totally vicious, premeditated, reckless attack by two men displaying complete and utter disregard for the consequences, or the serious (fatal) injuries it would cause, by using offensive weapons on an innocent, defenceless, unarmed victim.'

Having described a similar, if not exact, account of the events and subsequent proceedings relating to this case, I will now describe the account given by the defence counsel and his interpretation of the same events and resulting outcome, regarding the death of the victim.

He began with, 'It appears that while looking for a flatmate in order to share the costs of running his house, the younger of the two cousins was contacted regarding same and subsequently agreed to move in. The boys led a fairly quiet life, considering their relatively young ages. It also did not go unnoticed by the boys that their downstairs neighbour, the aforesaid victim, James Miller, was indeed renowned for having a bit of a reputation in the area as what can only be described as a local hardman and was certainly not the kind of person whom you would go out of your way to get involved with. As a result, the boys made a point of deliberately steering clear of him at all times and trying to maintain a quiet and unobtrusive lifestyle. However, on the particular day of the events leading up to the unfortunate episode that brings us to court today, the younger of the two accused had left the house with his golf club, to go on to a nearby grassy knoll in front of the tenement building where he stayed, to practise his golf swing. It was whilst engaged alone in this particular activity that he was approached and subsequently confronted by the renowned James Miller, who lived up to his hardman reputation by threatening the younger man with acts of violence if he did not refrain from playing his music. During this episode of events, the second cousin had occasion to look out of the window of his house and observe the events taking place. On seeing the look of what can only be described as fear and obvious alarm etched across the face of his younger cousin, he immediately left the house to go to his assistance. In haste, as he made his way out of the house, he picked up the first thing he could lay his hands on, which unfortunately just happened to be a kitchen knife. There was absolutely no intent to use the knife, it was merely to act as a threat, or deterrent, against a grown, mature man such as James Miller, with a fearsome reputation and who was presently threatening his younger, terrified cousin. As it was, as he made his way towards the scene to confront Miller, he to, became embroiled in a heated argument, but was still trying desperately in his own way to defuse the situation amicably, without anyone getting hurt. Suddenly, and purely by accident, the younger cousin swung his golf club at the ball on the ground, missing it completely, but as a result of his action, he followed through with his swing and struck the victim, Miller, on the rear of his head, an action which caused James Miller to lunge forward. In what appeared like a physical attack by Miller, as he lunged forward at him, the second cousin reacted instantly by striking out with his clenched fist in a punching motion, while momentarily forgetting that he was holding a knife. As a result, the victim, Miller, was stabbed several times. The accused immediately regretted their spontaneous but accidental actions and responded by trying to give assistance to the victim, Miller, but to no avail. Both young men were, and still are, totally inconsolable with remorse regarding the regrettable and unfortunate events of that day and the fatal consequences as a result of their actions. However, m'lord, I would reiterate that these young men were deliberately placed in this unfortunate situation by the victim, James Miller, and his threats of physical violence coupled with his fearsome reputation in the area as a vicious hardman.'

One defendant was sentenced to two years' imprisonment and the other received 200 hours' community service, thrown in as an afterthought.

Now you're probably thinking to yourself, 'That's got to be a bloody joke!' but regrettably it's not.

Unfortunately, for us all, it's our so-called legal system! Which makes you seriously wonder, why didn't the judge just throw in some golf lessons as well?

Bargains Galore

. . .

Dae ye want tae buy some aftershave,
Some razor blades or toys?
Dae ye need some kiddies' clothes?
I can supply it for girls or boys.
Everything is a third of the price
And I'll deliver them tae yer door.
Don't ask me where they came from
And I'll promise tae get ye more.
Dae ye want tae buy a hi-fi, a video or DVD?
They fell aff the back of a lorry
And guess who found them? Me!
I can sell them tae ye dirt cheap
'Cause nuthin' in life is free,
But don't expect yer money back
Because there is nae guarantee.
I need the cash right here and now
'Cause I've an itch I need tae scratch,
I know a punter who's dealing drugs
And I'd like tae score a batch.
So make yer mind up quickly
Or somebody else will buy it
And if things get hot and you get caught
Jist remember, I'll deny it!

Anon

Did You Say a Raygun?

· · ·

A call was received at the control room, reporting an incident involving firearms.

The controller made several unsuccessful attempts to contact the duty armed response vehicle crew, and unable to gain any response, it was decided to contact them via their mobile phone.

After a few rings, the telephone was answered.

'Hello there, it's the force control room here,' the controller said.

The voice at the other end of the phone replied, 'Hello! What can I do for you?'

'Can you attend a firearms incident, regarding a man seen in possession of a shotgun?' the controller asked.

Whereby the voice at the other end of the phone replied, 'I would love to, but I can't.'

'And why not?' the irate controller responded.

'Because I'm a spray painter in a garage workshop and the only gun I have is a spray gun.'

This response was followed by silence from the control room and a red face for the controller.

Doctor's Surgery

· · ·

Everybody has been through this at one time or another.

You enter the surgery and there is a sign above the wee window where the receptionist sits, which states, 'Please stand back and afford each patient some privacy.'

Then the receptionist asks you, 'And what's wrong with you today, Mr Morris?'

Now, she is sitting inside a room by herself, speaking to you through a small window, whereas I am on the outside, standing in a crowded waiting room, surrounded by several other patients.

So I whisper to her what my complaint is, to which she responds by asking me to repeat it.

Now, I would see the point if she was going to prescribe something for my problem, but she's not!

She's just a nosy cow and looking for something juicy to tell all her pals at the next slimmers' club meeting.

Therefore I have a new way of approaching this problem and it's this:

I walked into the crowded surgery and approached the wee window, where she asked me, 'Well, Mr Morris, what are you here to see the doctor about today?'

I responded by blurting out, 'There's something up with my penis!'

The receptionist became very irritated by my response to her question and said, 'You can't walk into a crowded waiting room and speak like that.'

'Why not?' I replied. 'You asked me what I wanted to see the doctor about and I just told you!'

'But you have caused embarrassment to some of the other patients in the waiting room,' she replied. 'You should have just said you had something wrong with your nose, or something like that, and then you can discuss the problem further with the doctor in private.'

'Well, maybe you shouldn't have asked me what I wanted to see the doctor about in front of a crowded waiting room of strangers,' I replied.

However, I then walked out of the surgery, waited a few moments, then re-entered, where I made my way up to the receptionist's window.

She looked at me and gave a smug grin, before saying, 'What would you like to see the doctor about today?'

I decided to play her game.

'I have something up with my nose!' I replied.

The receptionist nodded and gave me an approving smile, pleased that I had taken her advice.

'And what is it that is wrong with your nose, Mr Morris?' she asked, rather condescendingly.

Too which I couldn't resist replying, 'I have a problem when I'm pissing out of it!' much to the delight and laughter of the waiting room.

Upper-class Neds

· · ·

It would appear that after some research, the neds from the Paisley area are more fussy and hard to please than anywhere else in Strathclyde.

Such was the case when a car owner parked his vehicle in a car park near to the town centre while he went Christmas shopping.

What a shocking surprise he received on his return a few hours later – his car door lying open, his passenger window smashed and his car ransacked.

However, the biggest surprise for the car owner was the fact that his precious radio/cassette had been removed from the dashboard and left on the roof of his car with a note attached to it which stated: 'YOUR FUCKING STEREO'S NOT WORTH A SHIT . . . MERRY XMAS!'

I love it!

A ned who steals to a high standard and is not satisfied with any old crap!

Supervisors

...

When the body was first developed, all parts wanted to be the boss.

The brain insisted, 'Since I control everything and do all the thinking, I believe that I should be the boss.'

The feet said, 'Since we carry "man" wherever he wants to go, we should be the boss.'

The hands said, 'Since we do all the work and earn all the money to keep the rest of you going, we should be the boss.'

The eyes then staked their claim: 'Since we have to look out for all of you, we should be the boss.'

And so it went on, with the heart, the ears and finally . . . the bum. The other parts all laughed at the thought of it. Imagine the bum thinking he could be the boss!

Due to the others' hurtful remarks, the bum got mad and refused to function.

As a result, the brain became feverish, the eyes crossed and ached, the legs got wobbly and the stomach became bloated and sore.

All of them pleaded with the brain to relent and allow the bum to be boss.

Under pressure, the brain agreed.

All the other parts got back down to doing their work and the bum simply took over and became the boss and passed a load of crap!

Moral of the story?

You don't have to be a brain to be a boss . . . only a bum!

The Bar Officer

· · ·

The door to the station opened and in walked an obnoxiously loud and very unattractive, snarling-faced woman with two young children, who she was verbally and physically abusing all the way up to the desk.

The elderly senior police officer on desk duty greeted her with the following: 'Good morning ma'am. Nice children you have – are they twins?'

The ugly woman immediately stopped her verbal and physical abuse of them and turned her attention to the police officer.

'Christ no! . . . They're no' twins . . . The oldest is nine and the younger one is seven.' she replied, before asking in an aggressive manner.

'Whit the hell would possibly make you think they were twins? . . . Are you blind or just stupid? . . . You don't really believe they look alike. Do you?'

'No!' replied the elderly officer shaking his head.

'But what I find even harder to believe is the fact that you could have been laid twice!'

Offer a Lift Home?

. . .

At a recent party being held in a local bowling club by a retiring police officer – which just so happened to be well attended by his many colleagues, all looking for a drink on the 'auld yin' – a young probationer policewoman, who had consumed several drinks over a very short period of time that evening, showed off her well-rehearsed party trick of putting her full hand into her mouth, up to her wrist.

There wasn't a man or woman in the club that night who wasn't suitably impressed.

Subsequently, after performing this fantastic, nay, *amazing* feat, she received offers from several of her male colleagues – and two female officers – of a lift home that night.

Isn't it amazing how a little thing like that can impress so many people?

Now, I'm not boasting, but not to be outdone by a young female probationer, I would just like to make you aware that I can bite my big toe, on either foot.

However, I cannot remember ever being offered a lift home from anybody.

Am I missing something here?

Breastfeeding Awards

· · ·

'Harry boy! It's me, Donnie. I cannot believe it! After you giving me absolute pelters for trying to enrol you into my latest public service of the breastfeeding support classes, I have come across this leaflet at the local gym. It's called the Breastfeeding Welcome Award and is an award given to public places that welcome breastfeeding mothers and their children. Now, wait for it – places that meet the award criteria receive a certificate and stickers to display.'

Donnie then informed me that he had applied for an inspection, to see if his new conservatory meets with the criteria, or will he have to fit venetian blinds all round?

These places must also employ caring staff who are welcoming and helpful to breastfeeding mothers and who are displaying a 'Breastfeeding Welcome' logo.

'Does that not describe me to a tee?' Donnie asked. 'And no specification as to the sex staff need to be. Now, the logo is that of a young woman cradling a baby to her bosom and appearing to be breastfeeding it. Also, the staff must respect a mother's right to breastfeed anywhere, in the building or the grounds! And the breastfeeding mother must be left undisturbed, although staff – that's me – will respond in a positive manner if asked for assistance, e.g. supply a chair, a glass of water, or in my case,' added Donnie, 'give a helping hand! And how do they define a public place?' he asked. 'Anywhere that is open to the general public and where they have access, such as cafés, museums, shops, football stadiums, sports centres, swimming pools, banks, Donnie's new conservatory' –which he informs me is now open to the public – 'libraries, hospitals, on public transport, while driving a bus, health centres, in a church, during confession, dental surgeries, community centres, your own living room and even playing in goal for Hearts, if selected by the owner, Vladimir Romanov, etc.'

Now, a word of warning to all young mothers out there with babies whom they are breastfeeding. Does this new act not have a loophole, which is there to be abused by Donnie, a keen, eager and helpful member of the public?

And finally, the Breastfeeding (Scotland) Act 2005 states the following:

This Act of the Scottish Parliament makes it an offence to prevent, or stop a child who is permitted to be in a public place, or licensed premises from being fed milk in that place, or on those premises; and for connected purposes.

So the next time you are in the cinema, smooching with your girlfriend, wife, or someone else's wife for that matter, and you hear peculiar, loud sooking noises coming from behind you, don't be alarmed, it's probably just some wean getting breastfed! Well . . . Maybe?

Begin the Begin

• • •

A cop returned home after a long and arduous back shift, sat down in his favourite chair in front of the fire, turned on his TV and said to his wife, 'Quick, hen! Bring me a cool beer out the fridge before it starts!'

The wife gave him a puzzled look, but brought his beer.

As soon as he had finished it, he said, 'Quick, hen! Bring me another cool beer, it's definitely going to start soon!'

This time the wife looked a little angry, but brought him the beer.

After he drank this one down, he again said, 'Quick, hen! Another beer before it starts!'

The wife stared at him for a moment before blowing her top.

'You big bastard! You waltz in here, flop your big fat arse down on the seat, don't even say hello to me, but you expect me to run around like a bampot, serving you drink. Don't you realise that I cook, clean, wash and iron all bloody day long while you're out?'

The cop looked at her, sighed and said, 'It's started!'

The Office Cleaner

· · ·

From *The Adventures of Harry the Polis*

(*Harry arrived at work and heard someone talking out in the front office.*)

HARRY: Who is that out in the front office?
SPOOK: Dat's da new cleaning lady.

(*Harry walks out to the front and immediately recognises her as an old flame of his.*)

HARRY: Thelma Moffat!
THELMA: Crikey, Harry the Polis!

(*They both cuddle each other.*)

HARRY: What are you in here for, soliciting?
THELMA: You must be joking, I'd need to pay the punters. No, I'm your new cleaner.
HARRY: I thought you'd be a woman of leisure.
THELMA: And I thought you'd be retired by now!
HARRY: No way, there's a few miles left in my engine!

(*Harry reached out and grabbed her around the waist and gave her a gentle squeeze.*)

THELMA: Well, if you want a service, go to a church!

Nursing Homes

· · ·

I was watching a programme on television recently regarding the ill-treatment of the elderly and infirm while in the residential care of a nursing home.

Now you are bound to get the occasional isolated incident in the news, where an inexperienced carer loses his or her patience with an elderly person, but in general, I would say that the majority of the homes were extremely well managed with a caring, patient staff.

I regard care homes now as a necessity in today's society, particularly when you get to a stage where you are unable to look after yourself and thus become a danger not only to yourself but to others.

Simple things become more difficult as we get older and forgetfulness is one of the major problems, like forgetting to turn off the bath water, or switch off the cooker, or even just forgetting to eat.

That is why we need to have a place for them to go, in order to be cared for and looked after, but, more importantly, to feel safe!

A friend contacted me recently and related the circumstances of his widowed father's behaviour, as a result he'd been admitted into a care home.

It was strange for his father for the first few days trying to adjust, but after almost a week he seemed to be settling in to his new surroundings.

On a visit, my friend said to his father, 'You seem more settled today, Dad, are you beginning to like it?'

'I am, son, and I'm not. I'll tell you for why,' his dad

replied. 'I was coming out the bath the other night and the young nurse gave me a hand and helped dry me off, after which she helped me on with my clean pyjamas and slippers, before sitting me down with a cup of tea and toast. About half an hour later, I was getting into my bed, when an older nurse came into my room to check on me. "You didn't comb your hair, Mr Brown?" she said. At that, she leaned over and took my comb from my bedside cabinet and proceeded to comb it. "There you are, Mr Brown, you definitely look more handsome now!" At that she began to tuck me in, when she noticed a wee bump in the bed. "What's this, Mr Brown? What do we have here?" she said, as she put her hand under the covers and grabbed hold of my semi-erect penis. "We can't let this go to waste." And at that she began to masturbate me—'

My friend interrupted him at this point: 'Well, there you go, Dad. That can't be all bad! A carer who provides you with the occasional sexual favour!'

'Aye, but there's more, son. I'm not finished with my story yet,' his dad replied.

'OK then. Carry on with it,' my friend said.

'Right! Next morning, I got up out of bed, jumped into my Zimmer frame and was slowly making my way along the corridor to the dining room for my breakfast, when my pyjamas fell down to my ankles, tripping me up and causing me to fall over my Zimmer frame, with my bare arse sticking up in the air.'

'Well, these things happen, Dad. It's just an accident!' my friend said.

His dad put his hand up to his face and said, 'Hold it,

son! I'm not finished yet. Anyway, while I'm lying there totally helpless with my bare arse sticking up in the air in this embarrassing position, a big male nurse appeared from nowhere and sexually abused me from behind!'

My friend was gobsmacked for a few moments, as he tried to come to terms with what his dad had just told him, and at the same time he was trying desperately to think of a suitable explanation to give for it.

'Well, Dad, you enjoyed being masturbated by the nurse last night and today, well, you were buggered. Sometimes you've just got to take the good with the bad.'

Whereupon his dad replied, 'That's very true, son. But let's face it . . . I'm lucky if I get an erection twice a year . . .Whereas, I fall down at least three times a bloody day!'

Midlife Crisis

• • •

My former colleague met with me for a drink one day and told me he was recently talking with his wife and said, 'Honey, twenty-five years ago, we had a one-bedroom apartment, a second-hand car, we shared a sofa bed and watched a portable black and white TV, but I got to sleep every night with a hot twenty-five-year-old buxom blonde. Twenty-five years on, having worked my way up through the ranks, we have a detached bungalow, two top-of-the-range Mercedes cars in the driveway, we share a super-king-size-bed and have a forty-eight-inch plasma screen TV, but now I'm sleeping with a fifty-year-old woman. It seems to me like you are not holding up your side of things!'

His wife is a very reasonable woman, so she said, 'Tell you what, darling – if it makes you feel better, you go out and find yourself a hot twenty-five-year-old buxom blonde and I will make sure you go back to living in a one-bedroom apartment, driving a second-hand car and sleeping every night on a sofa bed.'

Don't you think older women are brilliant?

They really do know how to solve a mid-life crisis!

Suits You, Sir!

· · ·

I was driving home after giving evidence at a High Court trial and I stopped at a pedestrian traffic light.

As I waited for the pedestrians to cross the road and the light to change to green, I looked over to my left at a charity shop for the Chest and Heart Foundation and there, displayed in the front window, was a beautiful double-breasted suit.

I couldn't resist the chance of a bargain, so I pulled in to the side of the road and parked the car to go and see it.

It was an absolute cracker of a suit and just happened to be the style I like to wear, so I asked the assistant if I could perhaps try it on.

'Certainly, sir, just go in there.'

At that, she directed me to a changing room.

Once inside, I quickly slipped off my trousers and tried on the suit . . . It was a perfect fit and very smart looking; I felt really good in it.

'I'll take it, hen,' I informed the assistant.

I then returned to my car and continued my journey home, where I couldn't wait to show it off to my missus.

'Look, darling! Check this out – it fits me perfect and it was only fourteen pounds out the charity shop down the road . . . What do you think, is it not a beauty? In fact it's not unlike the one I have in my wardrobe, and I paid a fortune for that, as you know.'

At that I slid my wardrobe door open to compare it with my own one.

'Where's my suit?' I asked, turning around to look at my

missus, who was trying to quietly slink out of the room unnoticed.

Then the penny dropped and I asked her again, with a more serious tone of authority in my voice: 'Marion! Where's my suit?'

She turned to look at me, fluttered her eyelashes and said, 'I'm afraid to say, but you're holding it, darling.'

WPC Blonde

• • •

The door of the writing room was thrown open and my female police colleague entered and began ranting and raving.

'That's it! I'm fed up with every male chauvinistic pig in this office who assumes that because you are a blonde female, you are a dim-witted bimbo, totally stupid, daft, simple, idiotic, dumb, or naïve!'

She then paused for a moment to calm down, then asked me, 'You don't think I'm like that, do you, Harry?'

To which I promptly responded, 'Don't be so ridiculous . . . ya silly cow!'

Hello There

· · ·

I was out with the missus today, doing the weekly shopping, when an elderly man, smart in appearance, approached me in the supermarket, all smiling as if he knew who I was, and seemed to be really pleased to see me.

I was quite delighted at the thought of being recognised by him for whatever reason, but slightly embarrassed that I couldn't remember who he was.

'How are you doing? I hardly recognised you there,' he remarked.

'Is that so?' I said.

'Most definitely, you've altered your appearance so much. Your hair looks a different colour, you appear much shorter than you were before and I see you're not wearing your glasses any more. What the hell is going on with you, Brown?'

I looked at him standing there, looking back at me intently, genuinely believing he knew me and said, 'I'm sorry to disappoint you, sir, but I'm not, Mr Brown, I'm Harry Morris!'

To which he responded, 'Bloody amazing – so you've even changed your name!'

Accidents Happen

· · ·

I was on a 'speed computer' course, whereby two unmarked cars were occupied by four police officers in each and fitted out with the new, sophisticated VASCAR unit.

Now the VASCAR unit is short for 'visual average speed computer and recorder' and, in a simplified explanation, it records the time it takes to cover a measured distance and the computer then works out the average speed that the vehicle was being driven at.

Both cars were supervised, with an inspector in one and a sergeant in the other.

It was nearing the end of our working day and the front police car, which was occupied by the inspector, was hurtling down the M8 motorway at a speed well in excess of the 70mph limit and was closely pursued by the 'chasing' second car, whose front-seat passenger was performing the duty of operating the VASCAR to accurately record the average speed the front car was being driven at.

All of a sudden, for no apparent reason, the front car swerved and careered off the motorway, down an embankment, where it overturned several times, before coming to rest upside down in a field.

Fortunately not one police officer sustained an injury in the accident.

At least, that was the case for several moments after it had come to rest, until an older, senior officer suddenly panicked and began shouting and screaming uncontrollably, 'Mammy, Daddy! Mammy, Daddy!' as he tried desperately to climb out of the overturned car, fearing it was about to burst into flames.

With his arms and feet flailing about in such a small compartment, the panicking officer accidentally kicked out with his right foot and then stamped with his left foot on the inspector's face, using his head and lack of good looks to prise himself upwards and out through the damaged car window.

As a result of the road accident, only extensive damage to the police car was sustained.

However, as a result of the panic-stricken police officer and his 'Mammy, Daddy!' actions, the inspector sustained a burst lip, severe bruising to his nose and a deep cut above his right eye that required three stitches.

However, the inspector was cheered up no end, and even tried to raise a smile, when he was informed by the police operator in the following car that their average speed before they lost control and careered off the motorway was recorded at 134mph.

I cannot reveal the true identify of the face-kicking driver, but can reveal he was thereafter nicknamed Mad Max for the remainder of his police service. Good, eh?

Deal or No Deal

• • •

One day my police colleague Jimmy Clark's father was out working in his front garden when a large furniture delivery van drew up outside his house and the driver and his passenger alighted from the vehicle and approached him.

'Here, faither! Are ye interested in a new carpet for the hoose? We're jist finished fitting out a big new hotel and have a few extra rolls left,' the driver said.

My colleague's father looked at them for a few moments while considering his offer.

'How much are they, son?'

The driver immediately replied, 'Seenz I know you, faither, gie me twenty-five pounds and I'll gie ye a roll wi' enough tae carpet yer front lounge . . . Deal?'

Mr Clark paused while he thought about it, before replying, 'Well, seenz I know you, son, and have clocked yer number plate and the name o' yer company aff the side o' yer van, I'll gie ye twenty-five pounds and ye'll gie me a roll wi' enough on it tae carpet my entire hoose . . . Better deal?'

A Lotto Revenge

• • •

I heard a story on the news the other day about a man who thought he had won the lottery, and as a result, walked into his boss's office, jumped up on to his desk, kicked his paperwork off it, then informed him in no uncertain terms where he could stick his job, only to find out later the big mistake of acting on impulse and not checking your ticket numbers thoroughly.

It reminded me of a story I heard about a policewoman who suspected her policeman husband was having an affair, and decided to try and catch him out.

As a result, she recorded the entire Saturday night lottery programme and the subsequent winning draw.

Later on that week, she went out to her local newsagent's and wrote down the winning numbers from the previous week and submitted them as her choice for the following week.

On the Saturday night, her husband was in the bedroom, preparing to go out and 'meet up with some of his shift colleagues', when his wife switched on the pre-recorded video tape of the previous week's show.

As he entered the room, his wife nonchalantly handed him the lottery ticket with the previous week's winning numbers.

'Here, sweetheart, I bought you a Lucky Dip lottery ticket. Hopefully you'll be lucky.'

As her cheating husband took possession of the ticket, she slipped her hand down and switched on a hidden tape recorder, while he stood facing the television, dressed to go out, awaiting the numbers to appear on the television screen.

As each number appeared, his eyes began to light up as the announcer reeled off the 'lucky' numbers on his ticket, one after another.

Having checked again that he had all six numbers, he shouted to his long-suffering wife, 'Ya beauty! Ya fuckin' beauty!

'What is it, sweetheart? Have you got a few numbers up?' she asked him, trying to sound genuinely interested.

'A few! I've got the fuckin' lot. I've won the jackpot!' he stated ecstatically.

'Oh, sweetheart, does that mean we're rich and can buy anything we like?' she asked him.

At which point he looked at her and his expression changed dramatically.

'No, sweetheart! It means that *I* can buy anything *I* like, 'cause I'm for the off. I was going to tell you soon, but I'm leaving you for good and I'm running away with Fiona Glenn!'

'Fiona Glenn? That policewoman who left her man and baby son? She's nothing but a tart. Every bugger in the Support Unit has slept with her!' she said.

'So what? I don't care. You're just jealous of her. We have been having an affair for several months and we're madly in love with each other, so you can keep the house and the car. In fact, you can keep the whole fuckin' lot, 'cause I don't need any of it any more, I'm rich and you're not . . . sweetheart!'

At that, he waved his 'winning' ticket in her face and

promptly left the house, no doubt to tell his new woman of his surprise win.

His wife appeared shocked and stunned at first, as she sat down on her seat with her face showing no expression whatsoever, for several moments, then the video tape finished and her expression quickly changed.

As she sipped on her glass of wine, she burst out laughing.

She allowed herself a moment to compose herself, before stating with total conviction and complete satisfaction, 'I've got a house and a car and now you don't, ya dirty cheating bastard!'

Danny's Dilemma
· · ·

After a game of police football, big Danny McQuade invited some of us back to a local howf in his area, on the Great Western Road, where he knew the elderly landlady.

We all arrived outside in Gibby's new red Datsun Bluebird and parked across the road.

As we entered the pub, Danny introduced us to Madge, the landlady, who promptly supplied us with a round of drinks, on the house, after which she informed us she was finishing early, but would leave us in the capable hands of her two daughters, Tracy and Lorraine, who would look after us in her absence.

We each took our drinks, ambled over to a table in the corner of the pub and sat down to enjoy them.

I was the first to get up and order another round of drinks, which Tracy placed on the tray.

As I went to pay her, she said, 'It's on the house.'

I then thanked her and returned to the table, where Danny winked his eye and said, 'Freebie?'

I nodded my head.

A short time later, Danny decided to get the next round in.

Up he went to the bar and said, 'Same again, Lorraine.'

Lorraine poured the drinks, placed them on the tray and as Danny was about to lift them up, she said, 'That's seven pounds forty please, Danny!'

Danny was stunned!

For a moment he looked as though he'd need to sit down and be force-fed a drink, but like the trooper he was, he put on a brave face, searched his jacket until he found which pocket he had hidden his wallet in and withdrew a ten-pound note to pay.

On his return to the table, he said, 'She charged me!'

'Well, maybe only the first couple were free. Never mind, let's just drink up,' I said.

A short time later, three gorgeous young girl students entered the pub and sat down at the next table to ours and we all began chatting together.

Duncan went up to the bar and ordered them drinks: 'Same again, Tracy, and three white wine spritzers.'

As he stood there with his money in his hand, Tracy placed the drinks on a tray and said, 'It's on the house.'

Duncan thanked her and returned to the table with the tray of drinks, where he whispered in Danny's ear, 'That was another freebie, big man!'

In the meantime we were learning more about the girls and the fact that all three of them shared an apartment in West Princes Street, nearby.

Time for another round and it was Gibby's turn, but to everyone's surprise, Danny volunteered. After all, it was his howf and he was hoping to get a free round and maybe get his money back for the one he paid for by mistake!

'Same again, Lorraine, and three white wine spritzers.'

Lorraine duly filled the tray with the drinks order, then announced, 'That's eleven pounds sixty please, Danny.'

All credit to him, Danny managed to compose himself and produce another couple of 'Queens' (ten-pound notes) from his wallet.

This was not only a shock to Danny, but also to the pictures of the Queen on the notes still in his wallet, who were now wearing sunglasses to protect their eyes from the light, having been kept in Danny's wallet for so long.

As he staggered back to the table, not from the amount of drink he had consumed but from the shock of having to buy another round, he was assisted to his seat.

The drink was flowing and the conversation became more friendly with the girls.

Gibby suggested that we all go back to their apartment and have a party.

'Good idea!' said the girls in total agreement. 'But let's get another drink first, to put us in the party mood.'

'I'll get it,' volunteered Gibby, as he rushed up to the bar. 'Same again, Tracy, and three spritzers.'

As before, she placed them on the tray and said the three immortal words we loved to hear: 'On the house.'

When he returned to the table, he couldn't resist telling Danny that it was another freebie.

However, Danny was too busy asking the girls if they thought he looked like David Soul, of *Starsky and Hutch* fame, but a better comparison would have been a 'lemon sole' of fishy fame.

The girls quickly downed their final drinks and suggested they would go on ahead, to tidy the apartment, put on some soft music, slip into something comfortable and prepare some 'Scooby snacks' for us to eat.

Gibby volunteered to run them along the road in his brand new red Datsun Bluebird, parked across the road.

'Is that yours? It's a lovely car, but no thanks, we're quite near, so we'll just walk it and allow you to finish your drinks in peace,' they said, appreciating the offer.

As the three girls left, Danny – or should I say 'David Soul' – decided to order up one last drink for the road.

'A bit of advice, Danny,' I said. 'Don't call the barmaid "Huggy Bear", I don't think she'll like it.'

Up he went to the bar and blurted out, 'Same again, Lorraine, minus the spritzers, and pour one for yourself.'

She promptly placed them on the tray and said, 'That'll be eight pounds seventy please, Danny.'

Poor Danny, he took us to a howf in his area and ended up being the only one paying for any of the drinks.

The Queen has never seen as much light for years.

'Never mind, Danny, I think we've definitely cracked it with they burds, that'll cheer you up a bit,' Gibby said.

As we drank up and prepared to leave, Lorraine shouted over, 'Say hi to Tom, Dicha and Harri for me!'

This didn't exactly click with us until we got outside and saw Gibby's new red Datsun Bluebird car with four flat tyres and a note on the windscreen which said, 'Sorry, guys, the party's off and you're not our type, but we did enjoy the free drinks and that's why we've left you with something to remind you of our time together. P.S. Enjoy your blow job, boys!'

Picture This!

. . .

Big John Wilson, an ex-inspector, after retiring from the police went into his second love, that of dealing in antique furniture.

In order to find that something different for his furniture store, he decided to go to Paris to see what he could find.

On his arrival, he met with some other dealers and selected several items that he was confident would sell back home.

In order to celebrate his new acquisitions, he decided to visit a small bistro for a glass of wine and sat down at the only table available.

Before long, a beautiful young Parisian woman approached his table and asked him something in French, which he did not understand, and pointed towards the spare chair, at which he invited her to sit down.

He then tried to speak to her in English, but she did not speak his language.

After a few minutes of trying to communicate with her, John took a napkin and drew a picture of a wine glass and showed it to her.

She nodded in agreement and he ordered her up a large glass of wine.

A short while later, John took another napkin and drew a picture of a plate with food on it and she nodded.

They left the bistro together and walked along the front, until they found a quiet little café that featured a small quartet group playing romantic music.

They sat down and ordered dinner, after which he took another napkin and drew a picture of a couple dancing.

She nodded again, and they both got up to dance.

They continued to dance until the café closed and the band began to pack up.

As they sat back down at their table, the young French girl took hold of a napkin and drew a picture of a delightful four-poster bed.

To this day, big John has absolutely no idea how she managed to figure out that he was involved in the furniture business!

Snap! Text

* * *

Bono, the lead vocalist of the internationally known band U2, is famous throughout the music industry for being more than just a little self-righteous.

He was playing a concert in Glasgow, when he asked the audience for complete and total silence in the hall.

Once everyone had gone quiet, he began to click his fingers together every few seconds.

After holding the entire audience spellbound for several moments, while continuing to snap his fingers he announced over his microphone, 'Every time I snap my fingers, a child in Africa dies.'

Suddenly a voice with a broad Glaswegian accent bellowed out from near the front of the stage, 'Well, fuckin' stop daein' it, ya fud!'

Order in the Court

. . .

True Stories from the Law Courts

DISTRICT ATTORNEY: Do you know if your daughter has ever been involved with, or presently uses, voodoo?

WITNESS: We both do.

DISTRICT ATTORNEY: Voodoo?

WITNESS: Yes, I do.

DISTRICT ATTORNEY: You do?

WITNESS: No, voodoo.

DISTRICT ATTORNEY: Voodoo?

WITNESS: Yes, we both do.

DISTRICT ATTORNEY: Who, do voodoo?

WITNESS: I do, and her too.

DISTRICT ATTORNEY: You do?

WITNESS: Yes, I do voodoo.

JUDGE: Would you both stop right there? I'm becoming totally confused with all this!

Heather the Weather

...

A truck driver stopped for a red light, when a young blonde girl pulled up behind him, jumped out of her car, ran up to his truck and knocked on the door.

The trucker lowered his window and the girl said, 'Hi, my name is Heather and you're losing some of your load!'

The trucker ignored her and continued to drive off along the road.

When he stopped at the next red light, the girl caught up again, jumped out of her car and ran up to his door, whereby the trucker again lowered his window.

As if they had never met, the young blonde girl said, 'Hi, my name is Heather and you're losing some of your load!'

Shaking his head, the trucker ignored her again and drove off along the road.

As he stopped for a third red light, the same thing happened, as the girl pulled up behind him, jumped out of her car and ran up to his door, out of breath.

The trucker again rolled down his window, whereby the young blonde girl said, 'Hi, my name is Heather and you're losing some of your load!'

When the light turned to green, the trucker revved up his engine and raced to the next traffic light.

When he stopped this time, he jumped out of his truck and ran back to the young blonde girl's car and knocked on her window.

After she lowered it, he said to her, 'Hi, my name is Billy and I'm driving a gritter wagon!'

Monopoly – a Game of Chance

· · ·

One late shift, the sergeant handed Ian Whitelaw a number of arrest warrants to enquire into.

That night, along with a colleague, he called at the house of a man known to him, who was wanted on a sheriff's apprehension warrant for failing to appear at court.

He knocked on the door of the house and it was eventually answered by the wanted person's girlfriend, who informed Ian that she had not seen him for several weeks.

Ian showed her the warrant and asked if they could come inside to check the house for themselves.

The female hesitated for a moment, before reluctantly agreeing to their request.

Once inside, Ian and his partner began a room-by-room search.

Finally, they entered the lounge, where they noticed a glass dining table covered with a large tablecloth reaching the carpet and a Monopoly board set up on it.

The Monopoly money was lying in two piles at each side of the table, with the dice out and houses and hotels set up in Pall Mall and Mayfair, etc.

Ian then asked the girlfriend who she was playing the game with and she informed him that it had been a friend from the previous night and she hadn't got around to clearing it away.

As he listened to her explanation, he noticed a slight movement of the tablecloth.

This prompted Ian to wander over to the table and pick

up a game card from the Community Chest, which he read out loudly: 'Go directly to jail! Do not pass go and definitely do not collect two hundred pounds!'

He then lifted up the tablecloth and smiled at the wanted person, who was curled up underneath the table.

Lack of Imagination
· · ·

Some women are just hard to please.

Take my missus for example: last Christmas I gave her a microwave oven and a toaster.

This year, I got her a new hoover and an ironing board.

She hasn't stopped complaining since.

It was her that asked for womanly things.

Ungrateful or what?

Always Check Under
the Helmet

· · ·

While out on patrol one cold winter's night, two police officers came across a young motorcyclist wearing a leather motorcycle outfit and full-face helmet, who had broken down and was in the process of pushing the bike along the deserted Fenwick Moor road, several miles from the outskirts of Glasgow.

They immediately pulled over to try and render some assistance and were informed by the young motorcyclist that the bike had just suddenly stopped.

One of the officers was mechanically minded and in a few moments had diagnosed the problem to be a frozen carburettor.

Simple enough to solve the problem if you have a kettle of hot water to pour over it; however, being several miles from the outskirts of Glasgow posed another problem.

Not to be dissuaded easily, his partner came up with another simple solution – pish!

He would urinate over the frozen carburettor and hopefully the heat from his urine would thaw it out enough to get the bike started and get our stranded young motorcyclist back on the road for home.

Without the slightest hesitation, down came his zip and he promptly produced his recommended 'tool' for thawing out frozen carburettors.

After the officer had performed this duty and done the needful, the young motorcyclist started up the bike and, thanking the officers for their much-appreciated intervention and subsequent assistance, roared off along the moor road.

Several days later, a letter was received at police headquarters from the managing director of a well-known biscuit company, wishing to extend his sincere gratitude to the two police officers who stopped and rendered assistance to his stranded young daughter after she had broken down with her motorcycle while travelling across the Fenwick Moor road.

I suppose the officer should be grateful that mobile camera phones were not around at this time!

However, his partner did send off an enquiry on his behalf to have his unusual carburettor thawing tool specially patented!

Private Places
· · ·

A young police probationer was out on patrol along with a colleague and stopped a motor car for a routine check.

While checking it over, the officers detected the strong smell of cannabis.

As a result, they removed the occupants from the vehicle while they conducted a thorough search of the car at the side of the road.

The result of the search proved negative, so they then began to search the two male occupants.

The young probationer, straight from Tulliallan Police College, volunteered to do the searching, having recently been shown how to go about it and aware of the places where drugs can easily be concealed.

He began his search at the bottom of the suspect's trouser legs and worked his hands up the way.

Having reached the point of no return, the suspect male became more uncomfortable by the young cop's probing hands.

Thinking that the suspect was deliberately pulling back from him, the young cop grabbed a hold of an obvious bulging package in the suspect's trousers and said with great pleasure, 'Gotcha! What's this, then?'

To which the suspect replied with a tear in his eye, 'That's my bollocks, sir!'

F*** Off!

· · ·

New medical syndromes are coming to light every day and society is making a conscious effort to understand those who are affected by them.

However, in one case that occurred several years ago a fifteen-year-old boy was detained for causing a disturbance, shouting and swearing in a shop.

The police were alerted and attended the location, and on speaking to the staff they were to learn that the youth continually verbally abused staff and customers.

'Right, son! What's your name?' the officer asked him.

'Scott— Fuck off!' the boy blurted out.

'What did you just say there?' the cop asked.

The boy tried to answer again before becoming aggressive: 'Scott . . . eh . . . eh . . . Fuck off!'

At this, the boy was taken out to the police car and off to the station, where his parents were eventually contacted after some colourful verbal abuse was spouted by the youth as the police attempted to obtain their details.

Eventually his mother arrived to collect her son, Scott Edwards, from the office and was informed of his outrageous behaviour.

To which the mother replied matter-of-factly, 'Yes, I know, but he doesn't mean to swear and shout. It's part of his illness. He can't control it.'

Thinking that the mother was attempting to make an excuse for her son's blatant cursing in public, the cop asked with a sarcastic tone in his voice, 'And what illness would that be then, that makes somebody curse and swear involuntarily?'

'Tourette's syndrome!' the mother responded. 'Why don't you look it up and educate yourselves, so that you'll know the next time?'

At that, she coughed and, while doing so, appeared to utter the word 'bastards' at the same time.

The officers for their part ignored her poorly disguised outburst and she was allowed to leave with her son, but not before he looked straight at both police officers and blurted out loudly, 'Fuck off!'

However, Tourette's syndrome would appear to be spreading around Glasgow rapidly, because whilst still a serving police officer, just about everybody I had dealings with would utter these same two words at me!

Including some of my shift supervisors.

(Oh, and the wife!)

Say Again

. . .

A couple seeking a divorce were in court and the judge asked the wife, 'What are the grounds?'

'A detached cottage set in two acres with a stream running along the entire back garden,' she answered.

'No, I mean, what is the foundation?' he asked her.

'Concrete, m'lord. It's built on concrete,' she replied.

'No!' the judge said, sighing and getting agitated. 'Tell me what your relations are like?'

'Well, both my parents are alive and he has an uncle and a cousin who live nearby,' she responded.

'Let me put it another way. Do you have a grudge, madam?' he asked.

'No, m'lord. But we do have a double carport which can take three cars at a push.'

Finally, in total frustration, the judge asked her, 'Madam, why exactly do you want a divorce?'

To which she innocently replied, 'I don't! It's my husband! He reckons he can't communicate with me any longer.'

Not in Jess

...

Tom Jess is a lovely fellow who, as well as being an active District Court justice of the peace, assumed the role of financial adviser to many serving police officers.

One day Tom strolled through to the front office of the Police Federation building with a dilemma requiring some urgent assistance.

It appears his niece and nephew were arriving from their home in England and Tom was, like all keen relatives, looking for somewhere nice to take them for something to eat.

Immediately, Margaret Dale the cleaner, who was more attuned to juvenile tastes, suggested, 'Take them to McDonald's, they'll love it there!'

'McDonald's?' Tom repeated. 'Is the food there very good?'

'Of course it is. Yer niece and nephew will love it, all weans love it,' Margaret assured him.

'OK then, Margaret, McDonald's it is,' Tom replied enthusiastically, before asking her in all innocence, 'Now, will I need to phone up in advance and book a table?'

Smokey Was the Bandit!

• • •

Smokey was the nickname of a serving police officer on my shift, and, like a few of the younger officers, he acted aloof and tended to flaunt his position.

One evening, he decided to visit his friend who had recently joined the police and was at present serving his second-stage training at the Tulliallan Police College in Stirling.

Smokey decided to take him and several other police probationary students on a local pub crawl in Stirling in order to show off.

Over the next few hours, numerous rounds of drinks were purchased and consumed before it was time to return to their accommodation at the college, and for Smokey to make his way back to Glasgow.

Having split up and gone their separate ways, Smokey got behind the wheel of his car and headed off down the motorway, which was relatively free of traffic at this time.

However, after a short while, Smokey saw car headlights approach rapidly in his rear-view mirror and the driver flashed his headlights for Smokey to move over into the inside lane and allow him to overtake.

Smokey ignored him for a moment, so the following driver began to make hand signals, jerking his closed hand back and forth in front of his face.

'So Ah'm a wanker, am I? Well, we'll soon see aboot that, ya bastard.'

With an act of sheer defiance, Smokey reciprocated and began gesticulating back, sticking two fingers up to the car behind, before proceeding to accelerate even faster away from it.

This action only antagonised the driver in the rear car, who immediately did likewise and sped up after him in order to maintain a close pursuit of Smokey.

This continued for several miles, with the following car driver flashing his lights and Smokey continuing to ignore him to move over, as he gesticulated with his middle finger and veered from side to side, straddling the lanes, to prevent his pursuer from attempting to overtake him, as both vehicles were driven at high speed along the deserted motorway.

Unfortunately for Smokey, as he passed another access road, he failed to notice a marked police car join the motorway, and within a very short distance he was now being pursued with flashing blue lights and loud sirens, culminating in him having to pull over to the hard shoulder and stop, although his first thought was to try and outrun them.

It turned out that the pursuing car was *also* a police vehicle, and as a result of his drinking and driving, Smokey was apprehended and conveyed to Stirling police station.

At his court case, Smokey was found guilty and following his subsequent police discipline hearing, he was required to resign forthwith.

It's just a pity Smokey took that one drink too many, or he might have realised the rear car driver was not making a rude gesture, but was in fact signalling him to put on his seat belt!

Knock It Off

· · ·

A ned was stopped for a faulty rear light while driving his car in the Balornock area of Glasgow.

The officers, after pointing out the fault to the ned, administered a police warning for him to have the fault repaired and were about to leave the scene when the young ned, not the brightest planet in the universe, volunteered the following statement: 'Thanks for that, mate. Ah thought yeese had stoaped me for displaying a knocked-off tax disc.'

Amicable Divorce

· · ·

I read this article somewhere and just had to tell you about it.

A 93-year-old woman and her 94-year-old husband, who had recently celebrated their seventy-sixth wedding anniversary, contacted a solicitor and applied for a divorce.

The solicitor was slightly puzzled as to why, after living together for all these years and having raised a family together they should wish to separate now, so he asked them, 'Why after all these years together do you want to get divorced?'

To which they replied, 'We were going to do it sooner, but decided to wait until the kids were all dead.'

Bible John Theory

· · ·

Several years ago, whilst a police motorcyclist, every morning I would appear at the rear of the Federation office, where my good friend Margaret Dale would make breakfast and we would sit and have a blether and a wee laugh between us.

Margaret got talking about how she believed she might have inadvertently saved some unsuspecting girls' lives during the reign of terror sweeping Glasgow dance halls, in the wake of 'Bible John'.

As a keen dancer, Margaret would frequent the Glasgow Barrowland dance hall, the scene of several of his victims' last sightings and subsequent disappearances.

Margaret's theory is that one night she actually danced with the suspect serial killer Bible John, so nicknamed because he would spout verses from the Bible, and while he was doing this she was repeatedly talking over him and not allowing him to get a word in.

As she said, 'He would've had to strangle me to shut me up, so much so, Ah think I bored the arse aff him and he got that fed up listening that he upped and left. Alone! Coincidentally, the Bible John murders amazingly stopped after that night. Here, Harry! Maybe he went home that pissed aff, he strangled himself instead?'

Who knows Margaret? It just might be true!

It's How You Say It!

· · ·

A young Strathclyde police officer was attending his training course at the Scottish Police College in Tulliallan and decided to phone home to check on his wife and children.

Each in turn spoke with their policeman dad, but his six-year-old daughter seemed the most eager to get on to the phone and inform her dad of a recent incident she'd seen near to their house involving the police.

'There were lots and lots of policemen, and police dogs and police cars and a helicopter, and they were all chasing after a car,' she told him in her excitement. 'Then the car crashed into a field and stopped, and the police car stopped, then the man got out of the car and ran away!'

'Oh! That sounds really exciting. So what happened next?' her dad asked.

'Well, the big policeman that was chasing after him just stopped running and shouted, "Where the fuck do you think you're going?"' She paused for a moment after blurting this out, then said, 'Is that what they're teaching you, Daddy?'

I Beg Your Pardon

. . .

Sadly, I learned of the recent death of a former colleague of mine, Eddie Weldon.

I was fortunate to have worked alongside Eddie on several occasions and we enjoyed some good times, relating old police stories encountered during our respective services.

One such story he told me was this:

Earlier in his career, he was working a beat that housed a local hardman who terrorised everybody in the area.

Threatened by his reputation, nobody was prepared to complain about him to the police.

After taking up night-shift duty, Eddie and his partner Ronnie received a call regarding a disturbance in a public house in their area.

On their arrival, lo and behold, the disturbance was being caused by the aforesaid hardman.

Without the need for witnesses, Eddie and Ronnie apprehended him on what they had witnessed themselves.

A few months later, they both received citations to attend Govan Police Court to give evidence for the Crown against their accused hardman.

It was common knowledge that in the interim period the accused had made personal visits to the houses of some of the locals who had been present that night during the disturbance, to remind them that they had better not be attending the court to give evidence against him.

Ronnie was first in to give his evidence and after he was

finished, he was about to sit down in the court when Eddie was called next.

As Eddie entered the courtroom, the accused looked around at him and stared as he was walking past.

Eddie immediately stopped and paused for a moment, before blurting out loudly, for all those present in the court to hear, 'I beg your pardon! I am not and I resent you making such a remark.'

The accused looked on in amazement.

'What is going on there? What's happening?' the magistrate enquired.

Eddie looked up at him and said with a straight face, 'The accused just referred to me as a "fuckin' wanker" as I was passing by him in the dock, m'lord.'

On hearing Eddie's outburst, Ronnie immediately jumped to his feet and added, 'That's the truth, m'lord, I distinctly overheard him.'

The accused in the dock looked over at Eddie and Ronnie, then turned towards the magistrate, before looking back at them.

'Did you call the officer that?' the magistrate asked.

Without the slightest hesitation, the accused, who was looking on in bewilderment, responded with an outburst: 'Did Ah *fuck*, ya bam! Ur ye aff yer heid or whit!'

'Indeed I am not and you are in contempt of this court,' the magistrate replied rather indignantly.

'Aw, fuck right aff, ya auld diddy! This is jist a total set-up with the lot o' ye,' the accused shouted towards the bench.

Moments later, he had to be restrained as he proceeded

to vent his anger at Eddie and Ronnie, who, for their part, stood impassively throughout the entire episode, with a look of innocence and total shock etched across their faces.

Oh, and he didn't miss the magistrate either with his abusive outburst, before being conveyed from the court, struggling violently, to be detained in custody on a new charge of contempt of court!

He's Definitely Dead!
· · ·

While training at Tulliallan Police College, I had occasion to attend the funeral of an elderly relative.

On my return to the college I was approached by one of the kitchen staff, who had noticed my absence in the dining room.

'Where were ye yesterday, Harry? I didnae see ye.'

I informed her I had been attending a funeral.

'Did somebody die, like?' she asked in all innocence.

To which I couldn't resist saying, 'Well, originally we thought he had, but at the crematorium he started banging on the coffin and shouting he was still alive, but by that time it was too late. The minister had signed all the necessary forms.'

I then left her with her eyes and mouth wide open.

The Place to Be!

• • •

This wee story was sent to me by an ex-colleague.

The boys on his shift were hosting a night for an older colleague who was retiring and at the end of the night the retiring cop, John Reilly, raised his whisky glass and jokingly proposed a toast: 'Here's to spending the next thirty years between the thighs of my lovely wife Rita!'

The following morning, he was sitting at the breakfast table with his wife and was saying how much he had missed her appearance at his retirement do.

'You know fine well with my strong religious beliefs I don't like to be in places where they sell strong alcoholic drinks and men swear and talk dirty,' she replied.

'Well,' he said, 'I proposed a toast to you at the end of the evening, where I said I looked forward to spending the next thirty years sitting beside you in the church.'

'Oh, that was very nice of you, John,' she replied.

Later the same day, Rita met one of John's drinking buddies from the previous night, who couldn't resist smiling and saying, 'John gave a wonderful toast to you last night, Rita.'

'So I believe,' she replied. 'I was a little surprised when he told me, because he's only done it three times in the last five years. Once he fell asleep, once he took cramp getting down on his knees, and the last time I had to pull him by the ears just to make him come.'

Odd One Out

● ● ●

At the beginning of my involvement with a Scottish folk band, we had managed to secure a last minute Hogmanay gig up near Aviemore.

I didn't have enough time with the band to secure any changes in appearance and stage plan, so I just went along with their present stage set-up.

Finding the location of the venue and getting there also proved a big problem, due to heavy snowfall covering the roads.

Once we were in the area, we came across a telephone box out in the middle of nowhere and used it to call our booking agent, who directed us along a snowbound, treacherous road for about another mile, where we were to look out for a village hall-type building, where he would be waiting, flashing the lights on and off to direct us in.

Eventually we saw the flashing lights and like moths we were attracted to this wooden barn-type building, adorned inside with colourful ceiling decorations, neatly laid-out tables and chairs and a large decorated Christmas tree up on one side of the stage.

The organiser assured us that the people would come.

We quickly set up our equipment and sorted out our sound check, prior to changing into our stage gear of colourful tartan kilts and tartan feileadh-mhors.

Ian, the lead vocalist, cheered us up by informing us that he had two bottles of single malt whisky in his bag, and was saving them for us all to drink and bring in the New Year.

Apparently his wife had bought them from an unknown man at the local market, who had sold them both to her for only £20, a price that an ecstatic Ian described as a 'steal'.

This news boosted everyone for about five minutes, then we suffered another setback, when Rob announced that the black plastic bag he was carrying, and which he believed held his tartan stage gear, turned out to be a bag containing his family's dirty washing.

As a result, by the time the audience had filtered in and we were about to take the stage, neatly attired in our colourful tartan stage gear, Rob took centre stage in a dreadfully crushed, bright-pink shell suit belonging to his wife.

'Don't worry, boss, nobody will notice!' Rob said.

'Nobody will notice? The entire blind population of Scotland couldnae fail to notice you!'

However, desperate times call for desperate measures, so we took to the stage wearing dark glasses, to hide our embarrassment at Rob's appearance, out front looking like Zippy from the childrens TV programme *Rainbow*, and began our performance, which, by all accounts, went reasonably well up until the next obstacle appeared, when we all stopped to celebrate and toast the bells of the New Year with our audience.

Ian grabbed one of his whisky bottles and opened it up to take the first slug from it as we all stood around in anticipation of our turn.

Glug, glug, glug! Suddenly his face changed and became distorted, as he swirled the amber liquid around his gums, before spraying the contents of his mouth all over us.

'Bastard!' he remarked before putting the bottle to his

lips and having another slug to confirm it to his taste buds. 'Bastard! It's bloody cauld tea!'

He quickly grabbed hold of the other one and, just like the first, it contained cold Typhoo.

With disappointment looming amongst us, and an audience who were not prepared to share their drink with us, I decided to play on and get finished in time to get over to our B&B in order to maybe get an alcoholic drink from our host.

As the finale heated up and the excitement grew among us and our audience, we raised the tempo on stage for our big finish, which arrived unexpectedly prematurely.

Unfortunately, with all the jumping about and vibration going on in the hall, the very large Christmas tree to one side of us fell over – *timber!* – and went crashing off the stage and blootered several in the audience who had been dancing at the front.

As if that wasn't bad enough, it also ripped out the decorative coloured lights and fused the entire hall . . . along with our sound system.

Not exactly the grand finish we had rehearsed, but I bet they won't forget the last song – 'I'll Tell My Ma When I Get Home'!

So, out of a gig fee of £250, we had to pay our fuel expenses up there, £40; the hire of the PA sound system, £60; a bottle of Glen Orchy whisky, £24; and £48 towards the cost of our B&B accommodation, making a grand total of £172.

We headed back down the road the following day with a paltry £78 between six of us.

Who said you can't make money in the music business?

Getting Auld

• • •

Three elderly retired officers meet up at the police convalescent home in Harrogate in Yorkshire.

After a great first night of reminiscing they all went off
to their respective bedrooms.

Next morning at the breakfast table, they were
discussing who had the worst health problems, when one
of them said, 'Well, I don't know about you two, but every
morning I have to get up for a pee and stand for twenty
minutes trying to coax it out and when I eventually start
pissing, it comes trickling out very slowly.'

The second old cop said, 'That's nothing. Every
morning I have to go for a shit and end up sitting on the
toilet pan for over an hour because of my constipation. It's
absolutely murder.'

The third old cop just looked at the both of them and
said, 'I wish I had your problems. See me? Every morning
at 7 a.m., I pish like a horse and I shit for Britain . . . The
only problem is, I don't waken up until half past nine!'

Applause!

. . .

I arrived home recently on a flight from Spain and as the aeroplane touched down on the tarmac, several of the passengers began to applaud ecstatically.

Can I just say to those passengers on Ryanair Flight 7843,

It's meant to do that! That's why they have a pilot!

What next?

Should we applaud the bus driver for dropping us off at our stop? Or maybe just the fact that he arrived at the bus stop on time!

Historic Bus Rides

. . .

Whilst performing a book signing session near Inverness, I spotted a bus going to Culloden via Tesco.

I can just imagine the chieftains: 'Right, lads, before we fight this lot, I've just got a couple of messages to get for the wife from Tesco.'

Balls Still Intact

· · ·

A cop arrived home to find his wife and her best friend in a discussion about the vasectomy her friend's husband had recently undergone.

'Don't tell me you've no' put your name down to have it done! You're a bloody disgrace for a man, Thomas Barr!' the friend said.

Her opinion, for what it was worth, was that a man's prized testicles were the equivalent of 'baubles' hanging from a Christmas tree – purely there for decoration purposes only!

Now, for someone like Thomas, who wouldn't even consider the thought of dressing a slice of fresh fish, this was a big decision.

'What do you think, kids?' the friend asked his assembled children.

'Hold it right there,' Thomas intervened. 'This is not up for debate. This is my private family jewels we're talking about here, so I think any decision regarding them should be made by me, thank you very much!'

'Do they just cut them off, Dad?' enquired his son.

'Don't be silly,' replied his older sister. 'Pauline's cat got neutered and it still has its balls.'

'How do you know that?' her father asked indignantly.

'Pauline told me, and anyway, I saw them for myself,' she replied.

'I thought Pauline's cat was a female cat,' he said.

'So did Pauline, until she took it along to the vet and he ended up neutering it. All the staff in the surgery were laughing at her for not knowing the difference,' she added.

'Well, if it hasn't got any balls there, does that mean Dad won't be able to kick it in the balls any more for peeing on his roses?' asked her sister.

At this point Thomas interrupted them: 'Right, I think that's quite enough about Pauline's cat and whether it's a he, she or it, so the meeting's over. As for my own personal belongings, I would just like to inform you all that I've grown attached to them and will be keeping them covered for the time being. And if at any time I ever decide to reconsider getting the chop, I can assure you all that you will most definitely *not* be consulted, or asked for your opinion, because pure and simply, they are both mine and I like them . . . decorations or not!'

He then stormed out of the room with his well-documented balls still intact.

For a little while longer, at least!

Bad Tempers

• • •

One night while out on road patrol, Eddie Oliver and his partner stopped a driver in his car for speeding.

The driver, who became quite irate at the thought of being stopped said, 'You must be mistaken, officer. I wasn't speeding!'

The wife, sitting in the front passenger seat said, 'I knew it. You're a fool and you're always speeding!'

The driver turned around and shouted at her, 'You just shut up, big mouth!'

Big Eddie was taken aback by the driver's outburst, but informed him that he was being charged for failing to wear his seat belt.

The driver responded by saying, 'That's not true, officer, I was wearing my seat belt!'

Whereby the wife yelled, 'I told you that. You never wear your seat belt!'

The driver turned around and threatened his wife, 'See if you don't shut up, I'm going to thump you!'

Not wanting the argument to escalate into violence, Eddie asked the wife, 'Does he always talk to you like that, hen?'

To which the wife replied, 'Not always. Just when he's drunk.'

Order in the Court
. . .
True Stories from the Law Courts

DISTRICT ATTORNEY:	'Doctor, before you performed your autopsy, did you check for a pulse?
WITNESS:	No, I did not.
DISTRICT ATTORNEY:	Heartbeat?
WITNESS:	No, I did not.
DISTRICT ATTORNEY:	Did you check for blood pressure?
WITNESS:	No, I did not.
DISTRICT ATTORNEY:	Did you check for any breathing?
WITNESS:	No, I did not.
DISTRICT ATTORNEY:	So, it is possible that the patient was alive when you began your autopsy?
WITNESS:	Not at all.
DISTRICT ATTORNEY:	And how can you be so sure, Doctor?
WITNESS:	Because his brain was sitting on my desk in a jar.
DISTRICT ATTORNEY:	Nevertheless, Doctor, could the patient have still been alive?
WITNESS:	Yes, it is possible that he could have been still alive and practising law.
DISTRICT ATTORNEY :	Thank you Doctor. I'll take that as a yes!

Permission to Slap?

· · ·

A former colleague and good friend of mine was Jimmy McNulty, who was a character in the police.

Small in stature, he was wiry, with a big heart.

He also had a wicked sense of humour, a great personality and a charismatic charm, with a voice that mesmerised, but most of all he possessed a desire and ability to be an excellent police officer.

I must confess to being impressed with his work ethic and his gritty persona – he would pursue an offender to the last, never allowing the bad guy to evade arrest and conviction.

This he would perform daily, whilst making regular attendances at various hospitals over several years of his police service for treatment to try and combat the spread of his incurable illness – cancer.

However, this condition did not deter Jimmy and with dogged determination he would lock on to a suspect like a terrier, latching on to their ankle and hanging on in there, refusing to let go, until he had collated and compiled the evidence required to seek justice and bring them to court.

I have many stories with regards to Jimmy, this is just one:

After another bout of sick leave, it was on Jimmy's return to duty that his senior divisional officer, having received numerous complaints regarding a lack of police presence and action, decided to offer him the position of 'village bobby' for the area, a position now referred to as local community officer.

Always eager to accept a challenge, Jimmy swept into the area like the new sheriff had arrived in town, determined to answer the many complaints of illegal parking and unnecessary obstruction by inconsiderate, negligent motorists, and the unruly behaviour of the local youths.

His first step was to enter a popular, busy diner in the area and announce to all within that if any of them had a car parked illegally outside on the street to immediately go and remove it.

Several regulars ignored Jimmy's warning and, as a result, Jimmy issued them all with parking tickets, which immediately stirred up a reaction with the locals in the diner.

Moving on, Jimmy then attended that evening at the local café, which attracted many of the young neds from the area, who tended to loiter about outside on the footpath and intimidate older members of the public by their very presence.

Gathering them all around him, Jimmy proceeded to warn them with regards to their future conduct and was about to move them on when one youth began to mouth off at him.

Jimmy stopped for a moment, asked the youth his name, and informed him to be quiet while he was issuing a warning to them.

However, the same youth continued to talk over him, so Jimmy issued another warning, but this time he added that he would slap him if he interrupted again while he attempted to make them aware of the rules.

But the outspoken youth ignored his warning and continued with his rude and unruly behaviour.

Suddenly, Jimmy raised his arm and swiftly slapped the youth across his face, just like he'd said he would.

The youth received such a fright by this action that he immediately fell to the ground.

All the other youths were astounded by this sudden and aggressive action by the 'new' polis.

Jimmy then looked down at him and said, 'I warned you to keep quiet while I'm speaking.'

As for the youth on the receiving end of the slap, he looked up and replied, 'Ya dirty big bastard, you're getting done for that!'

To which Jimmy said, 'Right, that's it. You're getting the jail for a breach of the peace.'

And he promptly arrested him and conveyed him to the police station, where he was detained.

A short time later, the doors of the police station opened and in came the mother of the apprehended youth, followed by all his friends, who had witnessed the 'assault' on him by Jimmy.

She immediately relayed her complaint to the station sergeant, with regards to Jimmy slapping her son, coupled with the fact that she was accompanied by several witnesses who were present at the time.

The sergeant was astounded and looked over at Jimmy and asked if this was true.

Jimmy confirmed that the action he had taken against the youth was exactly as told to him by the young boy's mother and the witnesses.

The sergeant was totally shocked to hear Jimmy admit to blatantly raising his hand and slapping the youth in front of witnesses.

'There ye go, sir! He has the audacity to stand there in front of you and admit that he slapped my son. What right has he got tae dae that?' the mother said, before looking over at Jimmy and adding, 'Well? What have you got tae say about that, then?'

The sergeant then looked at Jimmy, seeking a feasible explanation for his unpredictable actions.

Jimmy walked forward to the mother and said, 'With all due respect, Mrs Scanlon, I was simply carrying out your very own instruction to me when you specifically gave me permission to slap your son should he ever mouth off at me again when I had an occasion to speak with him.'

'Naw Ah did not!' she replied adamantly.

'Oh yes you did.'

Jimmy then reiterated an incident involving her, her son and Jimmy, whereby she had openly given Jimmy permission, when dealing with her son again, to give him a good slap should he show any disrespect towards him.

Therefore he was only carrying out her instructions.

'That wisnae you Ah gave the permission tae! It wis a detective called McNulty that Ah said could slap him!' she said.

At that, Jimmy removed his police hat and looked straight at Mrs Scanlon, before winking his eye and saying, 'I'm just Constable McNulty now, but I specifically remembered your instruction to me that day, giving me your permission, and so I acted on your behalf.'

The sergeant heaved a huge sigh of relief, as Mrs Scanlon and her entourage of witnesses left the station, deflated, having reluctantly admitted to having sanctioned McNulty's actions.

As a wee footnote to Jimmy's character and his remarkable outlook on life with regards to his serious illness, I have to mention that when we worked together in the Crime Intelligence Office, we would often be out and about, whereby we occasionally spoke with some of our informants.

Jimmy would finish up by saying, 'Well, there's my card, if you hear of anything at all, give me a call.'

And as we made to walk away, he would stop and say, 'Here, let me see that card a minute.'

Taking his pen out, he would write on it and say, 'You better call his number, just in case I'm not here.'

Taking Your Turn

· · ·

A call was received at the police station regarding a man in an apartment house, armed with a gun and threatening to shoot himself.

The armed response unit arrived with a negotiator and tried to reason with the man, but to no avail.

However, during all the talk that went on, the police officers in attendance did manage to gain entry to the apartment and now had visual contact with the armed man.

'Don't attempt to come any closer or I'll shoot myself!' he threatened, holding the gun to his temple.

The police continued to try and talk the man round and tried to convince him to put down the firearm, but he still ignored their pleas.

Time for a little reverse psychology, as the police negotiator, deciding that the man came across as of low intelligence and a blatant attention-seeker, said, 'Well, go ahead then, hurry up!' and began to joke and have a laugh with his fellow police officers.

Whereby the armed man responded, 'I don't know what you're laughing about – you're next!'

Better than BUPA

· · ·

My long-term friend and colleague, Jimmy Clark, recently underwent some major surgery in hospital.

After being taken to the recovery ward and lying there in his hospital bed with an oxygen mask over his mouth an nose, he mumbled, 'Nurse, are my testicles black?'

The nurse thought it was a strange question to be asked, but replied, 'I'll just check for you Mr Clark.'

The nurse then went to the bottom of his bed and, lifting up his hospital blanket and gown, she gently took hold of his penis in one hand and his testicles in the other, and had a close look at them.

An observation we refer to as a 'right good gander'!

She then replaced them in their original position and covered them up with the blanket.

'No, Mr Clark. There is absolutely nothing wrong with them, they look perfectly fine.'

Jimmy then pulled his oxygen mask to one side, smiled at her and said in a slow but clear voice, ' Thank you for that unexpected thrill, it was just wonderful, but I would ask you to listen again, very closely and carefully, while I repeat my question: Are – my – test – results – back?'

Now! You have to admit, there are times when the treatment you receive from the National Health Service is very hard to beat!

However, I suppose BUPA would argue that this was 'private' treatment of a different nature.

Public Warning

. . .

Beware of Pickpockets on the Subway

Drunk Is No Excuse

. . .

A police car signalled a driver to pull over because he was wandering all over the lanes of the motorway.

The police quickly formed the opinion that the driver has been drinking and, as a result, one of the officers said, 'Sir, I require you to provide a breath test.'

The driver looked at the breathalyser and said, 'Can't do it, ossifer, I'm asthmatic, and if I blow into that tube, I could take a bad asthma attack.'

'All right,' the officer said. 'Then I require you to come to the police station and provide a blood sample.'

The driver shook his head and said, 'Sorry, ossifer, but I can't do that either, 'cause I'm a haemophiliac. If I do that, I could bleed to death.'

'Well, I'll need a urine sample then,' the officer said.

'Can't do that either, ossifer. You see, I'm a diabetic and would get really low in sugar.'

'Well, I need you to get out of your car and walk along this white line,' the officer said, getting annoyed by his constant excuses.

'Can't do that either, ossifer,' he replied.

'And why not now?' the irate officer enquired.

'I thought it was obvious, ossifer . . . 'Cause I'm pished!'

Signing Sessions

. . .

Whilst performing a recent book signing session in a large bookstore, I was approached by a tall, smartly dressed, shaven-headed young man, who called me by my first name, to sign a book for him.

I immediately recognised his face, but was unable to put a name to it, so I referred to him as 'big man'.

'What would you like me to write?' I asked, hoping to learn his name.

'Just put "Best wishes" and sign it,' he replied.

As I did so, he invited me to join him at a nearby pub for a friendly beer after I had finished with my signing session, which I readily agreed to.

A short time later, I entered the pub and, on seeing me, the big man waved me over to him.

As I stood sipping at my pint, I asked him what department was he working in now.

'I'm a postman, Harry!' he replied.

I thought for a moment and then asked, 'So, have ye left the polis then?'

He gave me a puzzled look, before replying, 'Ah wisnae in the polis!' pausing for a moment before continuing, 'Dae ye no' remember me, Harry? Ye gave me the jail for a breach of the peace and vandalism, for kicking my burd's door in! By the way, best thing that ever happened tae me – made me get my life sorted out and settle down.'

Needless to say, I quickly drank down my beer and gave my excuses before making a hasty exit!

Name Dropper

. . .

Two cops were out on patrol one day when they saw two men having a punch-up on the grassy area of a busy roundabout.

They pulled up alongside them, got out of their police vehicle and promptly separated them, at which point one of the men ran off across the busy junction, narrowly avoiding being struck by traffic.

'Right, what's your name?' the cops asked the other.

'Audrey Hepburn!' was the reply.

This prompted one cop to administer a slap to his head.

'I'll ask you again, what's your name?'

'Audrey Hepburn!' was the repeated reply, prompting a second slap to the head.

'Right, smart arse, you're getting the jail.'

They bundled the accused into the rear of the police van and drove to the station.

They took the accused to the charge bar, where the duty officer opened his large station journal to note the relevant details of the accused and the charge.

'Name?' he asked the accused.

'Audrey Hepburn!' came back the response.

'I'll pretend I didn't hear that . . . so we'll start again. Name?' he repeated.

Once again the accused replied, 'Audrey Hepburn!'

The duty officer looked at the accused, shook his head, closed over his large journal and, lifting it up, brought it crashing down on the head of the accused – *wallop!* – causing the legs of the accused to buckle.

'Take the accused to the side and search him,' the duty officer ordered.

As the cops began to search the dazed accused, they received the fright of their lives when one of the cops frisking him down discovered the accused possessed a small pair of firm, perky and neatly developed breasts.

'Er, excuse me, sir . . .' the first cop said.

'Yes! What's the problem now?' the duty officer asked.

'I think we are going to require the services of a police-woman,' the cop replied.

'A policewoman? How come?' the duty officer enquired.

To which one of the arresting cops replied, 'Because I think the accused just might be Audrey Hepburn after all.'

Order in the Court
· · ·
True Stories from the Law Courts

SOLICITOR: How was your first marriage terminated?
WITNESS: By death.
SOLICITOR: And by whose death was it terminated?

Ah . . . Bisto!

. . .

Once when my daughter Kimmy was about seven, she was at Sunday school when the young minister taking the class was explaining the story of Elijah the Prophet and the false Prophets of Baal.

He was explaining how Elijah had built an altar with wood and cut the steer into pieces, before laying it upon the altar.

Elijah then commanded the followers of God to fill up four buckets of water and pour it all over the altar.

He then ordered them to perform this feat another four times.

The young minister then asked the members of the Sunday school, 'Can anyone in the class tell me why the Lord would instruct Elijah to pour this water all over the steer on the altar?'

Kimmy put her hand up in the air and started waving it about to attract his attention.

'Yes, Kimmy?' he asked. 'What's your answer?'

To which Kimmy confidently replied, 'To make the gravy!'

Nice Thought

• • •

One of the biggest issues that got to me as a police officer, and earned me a certain amount of ribbing from my colleagues, was at refreshment time, when I would sit down with the other members of my shift and take out my sandwich box, because I never knew what to expect.

My sandwiches were always better than the norm, but it was the fancy wrapping that caught the eye, as I would take them out from my box to find them all neatly wrapped in a very colourful, seasonal Christmas paper.

Fed up with the taunts from my colleagues about this, I decided around March one year to bring up the matter with my wife.

'Darling, you know I look forward every day to opening my sandwich box and discovering what goodies you have for me, but must you continually wrap them in Christmas paper? After all, we're three months into a new year.'

'I was only using up the wrapping paper that was left over rather than waste it,' she said, making her point.

'Well, let's have a compromise then,' I suggested. 'Use up the last of your paper to wrap my sandwiches in, but for goodness' sake, promise me you'll take down the Christmas tree for me coming back from work!'

Desperate Dermott

. . .

Every now and again, someone takes you seriously and writes to you, looking for you to provide them some of your expert advice. This was one of those times:

Dear Harry,
I would be grateful if you would kindly supply me with your worldly, expert experience of life and provide me with advice for the following problem.

I am twenty-five years of age and have two brothers.

One works for John Brown & Company and is an ardent Rangers supporter.

The other is an inmate in Barlinnie Prison, serving eight years for rape and wilful fire-raising.

My father is a fine old gentleman, living off the illegal earnings of my two sisters, who are prostitutes working on the streets of Glasgow, where they both hold down good positions in the West End.

My mother is seven months pregnant to our next door neighbour and, because of this, my father is now reluctant to marry her.

Recently, I have met with a sweet, lovely and charming girl who is an ex-prostitute, having only taken it up in the first place to support her drug habit.

She is a wonderful, sweet girl and makes me feel really good and her three children, of whom two are black, call me dad.

My problem is, Harry, should I tell her about my brother who is a Rangers supporter.

Yours faithfully,
Desperate Dermott (Mullen).

Dear Dermott,
Difficult one to answer here, so can I suggest that you please write to Linda Robertson at the *Evening Times*, Joan Birnie at the *Daily Record*, or Lorraine Kelly at the *Sunday Post*.
   Yours aye,
   Harry the Polis
P.S. Please don't hesitate to write again, I'm here to give help and advice!

Order in the Court

· · ·

True Stories from the Law Courts

ADVOCATE DEPUTY: Can you describe the individual?
WITNESS: He was about medium height, with a beard.
ADVOCATE DEPUTY: Was this a male or a female?

The Sting in the Jag

• • •

This is an unbelievable story about how gullible some Glesca punters can be, but more about how they really believe they can pull off such a ridiculous scam and expect to get away with it.

Information was received about a gang trying to set up a big heist which involved the theft of several brand new unregistered Jaguar cars from the safe, secure premises of a reputable company dealer's showroom.

It was decided that to successfully set up a sting to trap them would require the involvement of several undercover police officers from a totally different force.

Four undercover officers from the Metropolitan Police were recruited to carry out the operation, with the knowledge that they would have absolutely no connection in Glasgow.

After a thorough briefing, highlighting the background of the case with regards to the main suspects and the information already collated, the arrangements were made to put into place the set-up, using the four main officers recruited from the Metropolitan Police, who would be known as Sid, Bill, Nick and old George Dickson.

How original were they names then?

Unbelievable as it may sound, these were the names chosen by themselves and, apparently having used them before with a certain amount of success, they were accepted.

Fortunately for their part, our wannabe big-time con men were so blinded by greed that they didn't have an inkling and therefore, unbelievably, never once suspected our English counterparts' involvement, or considered for a moment their ridiculous but very obviously assumed names and identities.

The sting was based around two 'Mr Big' characters, who boasted openly to the informant that they could provide, at a price, these high-powered, highly priced, unregistered cars, the cost of which would also include their guaranteed delivery.

Several hush-hush meetings were arranged between the big two and the prospective buyers, with the discussions culminating in how many vehicles Sid, Bill, Nick and George were prepared to purchase, the total cost, the expected method of payment being cash, and, last but not least, the location and date for their delivery.

Having been informed of the specific arrangements at the meeting, the undercover cops returned to their Scottish police colleagues to relay the information required to set up the sting.

It was agreed they would purchase twelve brand new, unregistered Jaguars at £5,000 each, half of the money to be paid on confirmation that the vehicles had been safely loaded on to the vehicle transporters, with the balance to be paid once the transporters had reached a certain location on the motorway, en route to their new destination.

The gang had also paid off the garage company's security, in order to have them open the yard gates and turn a blind eye during the forthcoming proceedings.

However, the gang required one of the Mr Bigs to accompany Sid and Bill to their hotel room on the night, in order to check the £30,000 cash down payment, prior to the OK being given to the second Mr Big, signalling the start of the hijacking.

Senior officers quickly set about arranging the cash down payment and presented Sid and Bill with it, to retain in their hotel bedroom while awaiting the arrival of their guest.

While this was taking place, Nick and old George were required to accompany the second Mr Big and his team of drivers to the garage location.

During these separate operations, both Sid and Bill, along with Nick and old George, were being tracked and all conversations being recorded and relayed back to the Scottish undercover and uniformed police officers, directing them to the exact location, to take observations and await the code word being broadcast, whereupon they would move in and arrest all persons involved.

The hotel room door was opened and the first Mr Big was greeted by Sid and Bill, who invited him in to examine and check the bag containing the first down payment on the deal.

Having counted the contents of the bag, he contacted his partner by mobile phone to confirm all was in order, and to start the next part of the operation.

Quickly and efficiently, the cars were driven out of the secure yard and loaded on to the transporter.

Having completed the second part of the operation, the transport drivers were about to move off for the next location when the code word was broadcast and the observation teams of police officers swiftly moved in and arrested everyone involved in the sting at the showroom and over at the hotel.

At the subsequent trial of the accused, when the circumstances of the events leading up to their arrest were revealed and showed how blatantly naïve and idiotic they had been to be duped like this, their obvious stupidity had rubbed off on their high-profile defence counsel, who tried to cover up for his clients' gullible involvement in the entire incident.

Cross-examining the undercover Metropolitan Police officers – in a closed court in order to protect their true identities – he unwittingly provoked a hilarious response among the police witnesses by having to refer to them by their operational identities, i.e. Bill (the old bill), Sid (the CID), Nick (arrest him) and old George (George Dickson, affectionately taken from one of the first police TV programmes, *Dickson of Dock Green*), all names instantly recognisable and synonymous with the police and an obvious reference to police officers.

It was also most noticeable how professional the Met officers were in giving evidence and how they remained perfectly calm under the pressure of giving evidence and were not easily intimidated by the defence counsel or their high-profile reputations – usually an extremely stressful duty for all police officers.

One particular piece of the cross-examination that raised a smile was when a ridiculous scenario was suggested by the defence counsel and directed at 'Bill' in the witness box, whereby it was alleged that it was his intention and that of his colleagues involved in the operation, Sid, Nick and George, to double-cross the accused and retain the money for themselves.

Bill answered the defence agent's allegation, by stating that due to working regularly with accused clients, the defence counsel was beginning to think and talk like them.

However, he and his colleagues were dedicated police officers performing a specific duty and as such, they never forgot who they were, even when working closely alongside accused persons such as those in the dock.

The defence counsel, frustrated by the clever, precise and unruffled replies, coupled with a lack of any relevant and pertinent defence evidence, very quickly returned to his table in the centre of the court and sat back down, dejected and somewhat deflated by the expert police witness's sharp response.

After the accused were found guilty and informed of their custodial sentence, it was hysterical to see their defence counsel drive off from outside the court in a Jaguar! How ironic.

. . . And no! It couldn't be!

Police Landscapes
· · ·

A cop I worked beside who was Irish came into work one day all excited.

'Sure, you'll never believe this, Harry boy. An old distant relative on my father's side has gone and popped his clogs and left me a farmhouse and an acre of land in his will.'

'Lucky you!' I said. 'Where is it?'

'It's just on the outskirts of Dublin,' he replied. 'I'm heading over on my weekend off to see it.'

That day, he phoned around and arranged the ticket for his flight over.

On the following Monday night, after our weekend break, I met up with him on the shift.

'How did you get on with your farm?' I asked.

'Sure, it was wonderful, I've even taken some pictures to show you,' he replied.

Later that evening, we sat down for our refreshment break and he enthused about his inherited property and produced the photographs he had taken of it.

'The farm cottage is going to require a bit of renovation and modernisation, but I can do that at my leisure. However, as you can see, the land round about it needs to be dug up and levelled.'

'That will be costly to do that,' I remarked.

'Not at all, Harry boy! In fact, it's being turned over and levelled out as we speak,' he responded confidently.

'Who's doing that for you?' I innocently enquired.

'Sure, the local constabulary are doing that for me.'

'How did you manage to arrange that?' I asked him.

'To be sure, it was me cousin Kevin's idea. He just made an anonymous phone call, stating that there was a cache of firearms buried on the farm grounds. Christ Almighty, have they not being digging it up for two days now and they're almost finished it already!'

An Honest Mistake
· · ·

An elderly woman called at the police station to report having lost the tax disc off the windscreen of her car.

'Has it been lost or stolen?' I asked her.

'Definitely lost,' she answered.

'How did you lose it, ma'am?' I then asked.

'Well, I was driving down the road, when it just blew off my window,' she replied.

'And where was it?' I enquired as to her location.

'It was on the outside of my windscreen,' she responded.

'No, ma'am, I mean, where did it happen?'

Then I paused for a moment, digesting what she had just said, and as I looked up at her she shook her head, looked me straight in the face and said, 'Yes! I now know it goes on the inside of the window!'

Don't Even Think It!

. . .

A man was arrested for shouting abusive remarks at two uniformed police officers on the main street.

He was immediately warned regarding his conduct but ignored the warning and was subsequently arrested and charged with the offence.

At the police station, he was informed that the circumstances would be reported to the procurator fiscal and after confirming his details, the accused was allowed to go.

Several moments later, the police officers involved were leaving the station to continue with their duties when they were approached by the accused, who had been waiting for them outside, directly opposite the station.

'Excuse me, officers, but you arrested me for shouting that you were a pair of stupid ignorant bastards, right?'

'That's correct, sir,' one of the officers politely replied.

'So, if I just *thought* you were a pair of stupid ignorant bastards, would you still have arrested me for it?'

Both officers looked at each other, aware of what was coming next: 'No, sir. We can't arrest anyone for what they might think.'

'Well, in that case,' the man said, with a smirk on his face, 'I *think* that you are a big pair of stupid ignorant bastards!'

At which point the officers immediately arrested him again with the same offence as before and said, 'You might think it, son . . . but what you *don't* do is say it!'

A Confession or What?

• • •

I received this from an ex-colleague regarding a young probationer on his shift who submitted his monthly progress report to his sergeant (line manager).

After checking it over, the sergeant was confused as to what action he should take and faced a dilemma.

Should he take him aside and counsel him, or should he pass his report on to the divisional CID?

The young probationer's report read as follows: 'I have been personally involved in a variety of incidents during the past month, i.e. assaults, thefts, indecent exposure and violently resisting arrest.'

Gee whiz, son, you've joined the wrong side!

David Who?

• • •

Police officers recovered a stolen car and, on checking it out, they found a stash of Davidoff aftershave and perfume worth several hundred pounds in the boot.

They contacted the registered keeper of the car and relayed the good news to him, whereby he said, 'Ah ken that's ma car, but Ah dinnae ken this "David Duff" fella that you're talking aboot!'

I Don't Believe It!

· · ·

A retired cop called the Police Federation to say that he had read in the newspaper that certain officers in England had received substantial compensation payments due to having suffered from stress whilst on duty, attending traumatic and tragic events. He was angry that the Federation had failed to contact him to advance his claim that he had to retire on medical grounds.

The Federation rep was unaware of his claim and asked him what his medical condition was, at which he stated, 'I've got PMT!'

This complaint from a man just happens to be another first for officers who've served with Strathclyde Police.

Chief Medical Officer

· · ·

I walked into the police doctor's office one day and noticed that he had a suppository sticking out of his ear.

'Excuse me, Doctor, but do you know that you have a suppository sticking out of your ear?' I asked him.

He put his hand up to his ear, pulled it out and said, 'Shit! The officer who was in before you has my pencil sticking out of his arse!'

Not Now, Thanks

• • •

Three Glesca punters entered their local pub and ordered up some drinks.

While doing so, they spotted a man who looked like Jesus Christ sitting at a table all by himself, and decided to each send him over a drink.

After the man had consumed his complimentary three drinks, he made his way over to the table where they were sitting to thank them all.

He shook hands with the first punter, who turned to his mates and said, 'Crikey! I've had arthritis in my hands for years and he's just cured it with one handshake!'

The man then shook hands and rubbed the back of the second punter, who announced to the others, 'Holy, holy! I've suffered from severe back pain all my life and he's just taken all the pain away with one handshake and rub. He's cured me!'

The man then turned to the third punter and as he held out his hand to shake, the punter jumped backwards and said, 'Bugger off, you! I'm on disability benefits!'

Think About It First

...

In January every year one Scot is remembered all over the world. I'm talking about none other than the great poet, song lyricist and writer of the most romantic words ever spoken: Robert Burns.

I had the honour of being asked at the last minute to step in and speak at a Burns evening in Larkhall.

Apprehensive as I was, I reluctantly agreed to do it.

Armed with my speech and my various bits of knowledge about the great man, I arrived at the venue to take my seat at the top table beside the other guests.

After several speakers had performed, it was now my turn, as the MC for the night stood up to introduce me to the seated audience.

'Right, gents. Our next speaker is from Glasgow and he has kindly stepped in at the last minute. The other guy who we wanted – and who we know is very, very funny – got offered more money somewhere else, so he cancelled us. I didnae book this next guy, so if he's not funny, then don't blame me.' He then put his arm out and introduced me as, 'Harry Morrison!'

The confidence of that intro was running down my legs as I took to my feet.

Mind you, in hindsight, I should have taken to my heels!

Racism or What?

· · ·

All the exaggerated fuss in the media over remarks made on the TV reality show *Celebrity Big Brother* reminded me of a story I heard in a church.

A black man moved into a new area and, being religious, the following Sunday he got into his best suit and made his way to the local church.

As he arrived there and was about to enter, he was stopped by the church deacons and politely advised against entering, before being ushered away.

The following Sunday, he again donned his best suit and headed along the road to the local church, where once again he was politely thwarted from entering by the church deacons at the entrance and prevented from coming in to worship.

The black man, disappointed by this treatment, made the long journey back home, where he knelt down on his knees and prayed to God: 'Lord, how come when I attend your house to worship, I am continually prevented from entering.'

To which the Lord replied, 'Don't worry about it, my son. I have been trying to get in there for years as well.'

Everything Is on Me

...

In the late 1960s I had enlisted with the Royal Engineers Territorial Army as a sapper.

During one of my stays at a training camp, I was stationed in Stirling, along with some of my old mates, Tommy Peebles, Jimmy Tucker and Ian Cameron.

After about a week at camp, Peebles came running into our billet, all excited, and proudly announced that his wife had just given birth to a new baby boy.

He was so ecstatic by the news that he invited the three of us out for a celebratory meal and a drink.

'Everything is on me,' he announced.

None of us needed to be asked twice.

We made our way into the city centre and Peebles decided on a very plush Chinese restaurant.

Whilst looking through the menu at the prices, I remarked that it was quite expensive.

'Don't worry about it! It's all on me,' he said. 'Money is no object tonight. Order whatever you want, my treat!'

He then promptly ordered up two bottles of their best wine and four large whiskies, to toast his newly born son.

'Right, Harry boy! What are you having?' he asked me.

'I think I'll have the sirloin steak, if that's all right,' I said.

'Give him a double helping of sirloin steak and mushrooms. D'you want mushrooms? You've got to. Give him a double portion of mushrooms as well,' he ordered.

'Whoa, Peebles, that'll cost you a fortune!' I remarked.

'Don't you worry about it, Harry boy, my treat, Money is no object tonight, so have what you like,' he repeated.

He then proceeded to order up double portions of chicken chow mein, fillet steak and king prawns.

The drink was flowing and the owner of the Chinese restaurant was rubbing his hands with glee at the prospect of receiving payment of our final bill.

Halfway through my double steak dinner, I couldn't resist reiterating to Peebles that this celebration meal and bevy was going to cost him a fortune.

'It's no' gonnae cost me a fuckin' penny, 'cause I've no' got any money!' he nonchalantly replied, while shovelling spoonfuls of chicken chow mein into his gob.

Suddenly, my enormous appetite deserted me and a feeling of nausea overcame me, as I sobered up.

I then stood up from the table, excused myself and made my way towards the front door, where a monster of a man resembling Oddjob from the Bond film *Goldfinger* approached me.

I quickly reacted by putting my hand into my pocket and took out the only money I possessed, a two-shilling piece, and promptly forced it into his hand.

On taking it, he thanked me and, opening the front door, he wished me good night.

Once outside I ran like an odds-on favourite winning greyhound at the Shawfield race track. Linford Christie would have been hard pushed to keep up with me, never mind catch me, as I ran all the way back to the barracks.

Early next morning, I was to learn at the parade that Peebles, Tucker and Cameron had been arrested by the local police for failing to pay their restaurant bill and subsequently causing a disturbance.

Although it was also stated that there had been four diners and there would be a full parade later, whereby, accompanied by the police, the restaurateur would attempt to try and identify 'the one that got away'.

Fortunately for me, all he could remember from the night before was the loss of pounds, shillings and pence!

This celebration night turned out to be an expensive affair indeed, as each of them were fined £30 in compensation and £10 for causing a disturbance.

As for me, I was later called to see the duty sergeant, who asked me, 'So how was your meal, Sapper Morris?'

'What meal would that be, Sergeant?' I asked him.

'The one that you failed to finish in the restaurant. Don't fuck with me, Morris, I saw you leaving the barracks with them . . . And I know you bunged the doorman. Fortunately, I also saw you arriving back early before the reported time of the trouble. So I will put it down to you having shown some good initiative and common sense. Now before I tell you to bugger off out of my sight for the rest of the day, just consider this. The two shillings you spent last night was probably the best two shillings you're ever likely to spend. You were very lucky.'

To which I replied, 'Yes, sir!'

But he was right – two bob for a sirloin steak with mushrooms, washed down with red wine and several large whiskies, mmmm!

Who Knows, Maybe?

. . .

An off-duty cop was on a night out and met a gorgeous girl in a bar.

Several drinks later, she agreed to go home with him to his apartment.

After making love all night, the following morning he asked her, 'Am I the first polis you've ever made love to?'

She looked at him intently for several moments, then said, 'You could be, darling, your face is definitely familiar.'

A Perfect Relationship

. . .

It is important that a woman has a good job with a nice car, secondly, that she is great in bed and enjoys making love to you any time, anywhere, and thirdly, that she owns a lovely house.

However, it's extremely important that these three women don't get to know about each other!

Shut That Door
· · ·

A young woman who'd split up from her boyfriend decided to advertise for a new flatmate to share the costs of her privately owned apartment and was pleasantly surprised when a young woman of the same age answered her advertisement almost immediately.

Having completed the formalities of an interview, the two girls appeared to get along fine and it was decided that she would be the one to flat-share.

Things went well for several weeks, with both girls taking turns at cooking and keeping the apartment tidy, until one day the owner returned home to find her flatmate in bed with a man, having sex.

The following day, the owner took her flatmate aside and pointed out the 'no men allowed in the flat' rule.

However, a few days later she returned to her flat to discover the same scenario, with her flatmate's underwear strewn on the floor outside her room.

The young owner immediately made her feelings known and ordered the man out of the house.

This provoked a heated argument with her flatmate, who wanted her boyfriend to stay the night, as they were about to engage in some bare-bum tig.

One word bothered another, until the boyfriend intervened and told the owner to politely 'fuck off': he wasn't leaving.

The owner had no alternative but to contact the police, and PCs Brian Davey and John McCall attended the call.

Having been made aware of the situation by the owner,

both cops entered the flatmate's room, where the male friend was lying in bed, pretending to be asleep.

'Right, mate. Wakey-wakey! It's time to go home,' Brian said, as he leaned over and gently shook him.

However, the male was not for wakening and continued to pretend to be asleep.

As a result, Brian was more 'frisky' in his wakey-wakey! method.

The young man then came to life and after exchanging a few words with the cops, he blatantly refused to get up out of bed and leave.

Such were his actions that his behaviour was tantamount to a breach of the peace and he was informed that he was now being arrested.

As the accused struggled with the cops, the half-naked girlfriend stated there was no way that they were taking her boyfriend out of the house.

She then ran from the room, slamming the door behind her, and locked it with her key and held it tightly closed to prevent the cops from getting out.

In the meantime, the boyfriend was struggling violently, resisting arrest, and so had to be restrained and handcuffed then physically held down on the bed.

Brian then ordered the girl holding the bedroom door shut to open it, but she point-blank refused, directing a few verbal expletives towards the cops.

At that, Brian grabbed hold of the door handle to pull the door open, but all he managed to do was wrench off the door handle, as the girl continued to use her full body weight to prevent them leaving.

Drastic times call for drastic measures, so Brian, not exactly a shrinking violet, took the physical route and punched a hole in the door panel and, with his next few punches, managed to burst a good part of it out.

He then looked to the side of the door, where he could see the girl outside, still holding on to the door handle.

While this was taking place, John was still wrestling on the bed with the boyfriend, who had become more aggressive, due to the fact that he was getting the jail and not his 'Nat King'!

At this point, Brian put his arm through the hole in the door and grabbed hold of the girlfriend by her arm and pulled her over towards the hole.

As he did so, he managed to get a better hold of her, whereby he physically dragged her by the head and shoulders up through the opening in the door that he had made and held her there until more police assistance arrived.

However, I'm reliably informed that it took several minutes for the attending cops to stop laughing and lend assistance, as all they could see when they entered the flat, was the girl's big bare arse and flailing legs, fully exposed, sticking out from the hole in the bedroom door!

I'm also informed by Brian, 'There's hope for us all.'

It's definitely the first time that a young female has ever tried to prevent him from leaving her bedroom!

Teething Troubles

· · ·

A stolen car was recovered by the police, and while searching it for fingerprints to assist them in trying to detect the culprits responsible, they discovered a set of false teeth under the driver's seat.

The owner was contacted, who immediately stated that they were not his teeth.

After some considerable inquiries by the officers dealing with the crime, they managed to trace the owner of the false teeth, whom they interviewed with regards the theft of the car.

The suspect vehemently denied ever being in the stolen car, or being involved in the theft of the vehicle, and gave the feeble excuse that he had lost his teeth a few days earlier and therefore it was purely an unexpected coincidence that they should be found in the stolen car.

However, the police officers carrying out the investigation didn't believe him and, as a result, they took great delight in charging him with deliberately lying through his teeth.

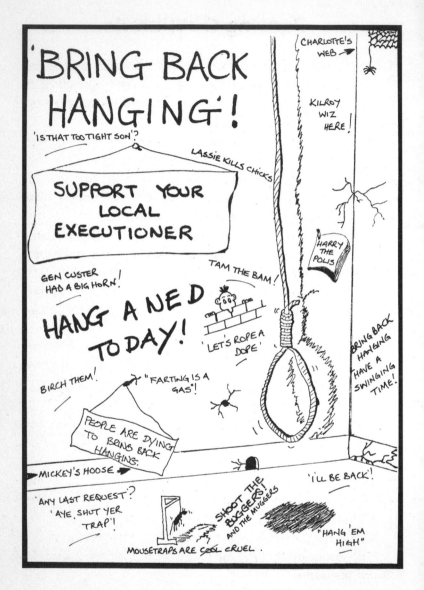

Passing Out Parade

. . .

During a passing out parade at Tulliallan Police College, the commandant was carrying out his inspection, going along each line of police recruits, when he stopped and asked, 'What's your name, lad?'

'Brown, sir,' the young officer replied.

'And where do you work, Officer Brown?'

'I work in the Baillieston area of Glasgow, sir.'

'And have you been involved in any interesting cases during your two years' probation?' he asked.

'Yes, sir, I have been involved in an attempted murder and was responsible for arresting two men on a charge of theft of a motor vehicle.'

'Good for you. That's what I like to hear.'

He then walked along the line a little further, before stopping again.

'Hello! What's your name?' he asked.

'Edward Gray, sir,' he replied.

'And where do you work, Gray?'

'I work in East Kilbride, sir.'

'And can you tell me about anything you have been involved in during your probation?' the commandant asked.

'Well, I chased after and caught a man for house-breaking and he admitted to the CID to a further seventeen theft offences,' he announced proudly.

'Good for you, son. That's what I like to hear!'

Further along the line, he stopped at another officer and asked his name.

'Wilson, sir, Thomas Wilson from Hamilton!' he said loudly and proudly.

'And what things have you been up to of interest during your past two years?'

'Not a great deal, sir. There isn't an awful lot of serious crime happening in the area I work, but I have been responsible for dealing with and clearing up a lot of petty complaints and domestic disputes,' he remarked.

The commandant stared at him for a moment and, leaning forward to subtlety sniff him, he then asked, 'Do you like to have a drink, Officer Wilson?'

Shaking his head, a rather cocky Wilson responded, 'Not just now, sir, it's too early for me!'

To which the commandant said, 'I wasn't offering, Wilson, I was bloody well asking if you had!'

Last to Know

· · ·

An inspector called at his divisional headquarters to enquire why he had not received the latest agenda for a forthcoming meeting, which he knew he was required to attend in the near future.

The excuse he was given was the fact that he would be working night shift on the particular date of the meeting, and someone else had been notified to attend and take his place.

'Hold on a minute!' he said. 'I'm early shift on that date.'

Back came the reply, 'Oh, has nobody told you yet? Your shift duties have been changed. As from next week, you're being transferred to a new relief and subdivision.'

And what was the subject of the meeting he was originally to attend?

Why, only the meeting being held for the launch of the latest police slogan: 'Investors in People', that's all.

Official Stamp

...

Following on from the last story, a serving police officer received a message that a letter addressed to him, was being held at the local post office depot.

The message also stated that because the letter had been posted without a stamp on it, he would have to pay an extra cost for the privilege of collecting it.

Off he duly went in full uniform to the local post office depot, where he was slagged off by the postal staff in the depot for having correspondents writing to him who 'deliberately' evaded paying postage.

On finally taking receipt of the letter, he was astounded to learn that it was an official Strathclyde Police envelope and it had been sent to him on official police business from the Strathclyde Personnel Department, Pitt Street HQ.

Now it's all very well to launch new slogans advocating 'Investors in People', but it might be a better idea if first the police became 'Investors in Postage Stamps'!

Who's a Pretty Boy, Then?

• • •

This, alas, is the sad tale of a cop who decided to do a good deed and take a homeless 'burd' home to the house.

Now before you let your dirty mind run riot, let me explain to you that it was the feathered variety.

It transpired that a canary flew into an open window and the lady house owner brought it to the police station and handed it in as found property.

As it was, there had been no reported loss of the bird, so the local community cop elected to take it home with him and have it adopted by his weans.

The kids were over the moon, and housed it temporarily in a cardboard box, while they all went off with Daddy to the pet shop to purchase a cage, bell, bath, mirror, etc., for their new lodger.

Unfortunately, while they were out, the wee canary escaped from the box and, while sitting, singing away, was promptly killed by the family's pet Jack Russell.

This was very heart-breaking for the kids, who were distraught and had to be consoled by Daddy.

However, as if this wasn't bad enough, the following day a lady called at the police station to collect her little sweety pie, having been told by the other woman that she had handed it into the police the day before! *Gulp!*

Love's on the Rocks

. . .

I was sitting in the hairdresser's the other day, waiting my turn, and I picked up a magazine with an article on Neil Diamond, the singer/songwriter.

Apparently he has just gone through a divorce from his wife and agreed to give her a final settlement of $150 million.

For that kind of money, I'd have married him, but that's not my point.

The point is that Neil is now reluctant to marry his present girlfriend Rosie because he doesn't want to lose any more money.

Now I could see the reason behind this decision if she had only been with him a few months, but it turns out she has been living with him for ten years.

As Neil states in his interview, 'We have a great relationship together and she is very caring and understanding with me and gives me her honest opinion, with regards to everything I do, in particular the new songs I compose.'

But further down the interview/article, he informs you that she is 70 per cent deaf!

Well, I'm sorry to tell you this, Neil, but it's no wonder she gets on well with you and appears to like every song you've composed and sung to her recently.

It's because she can't bloody hear you singing, that's why!

Now, poor old Neil has a backlog of about 4,000 songs he's composed and has had to pre-book the local recording studio for the next fifteen years to try and record them all on to CD before he pops his clogs.

The poor man's demented.

He doesn't believe he has written a crap song in the last ten years.

I'll let you into a secret, Neil: every time you composed a new song and played it to your live-in burd, she couldn't hear a thing and just assumed for the last ten years you've been playing 'Love on the Rocks' to her.

And as a result, when you said to her, 'What do you think of that one, hen?' she just took her eyes off her knitting long enough to glance over at you, nod her head and say, 'I love it, Neil, it's my favourite.'

So here's a wee tip, Neil! You'd be better playing her 'Crackling Rosie', 'cause apparently the 'crackling' part is about all she's hearing anyway!

Order in the Court

• • •

True Stories from the Law Courts

DEFENCE SOLICITOR: Now, Doctor, isn't it true that when a person dies in his sleep, he doesn't know about it until the next morning?

WITNESS: Did you actually pass the bar exam?

Hold On There

...

On his way to the post office, an elderly man suffered a heart attack, collapsed and died outside the door.

Donnie Henderson was the nearest cop to the location and attended to assist.

While awaiting the arrival of the ambulance, the man's wife, who had been sitting in the family car in the nearby car park, waiting on his return, appeared at the scene to see why he was taking so long, and recognised him lying there.

Experience had taught Donnie that fainting was not uncommon in such circumstances and, as a result, he put a fatherly arm on her shoulders to comfort her.

Suddenly, the wife's knees appeared to buckle, but Donnie held her up.

However, her legs appeared to buckle again, prompting Donnie to tighten his grip around her shoulders and hold her more firmly.

As he did so, the woman looked at him straight in the eye and said in a broad Irish brogue, 'For Christ's sake, son, will you let me kneel down and say a wee prayer over me poor man?'

PC Humour

. . .

Just to prove that computers have a sense of humour, I relate a story sent to me regarding the computer network installed at divisional HQ several years ago.

The computer had many functions, including producing official letter headings, bearing at the top the name and qualifications of the then chief constable, John Hoddinot.

The only problem was, when the computer performs a spellcheck of his name 'Hoddinot', it automatically changes it to 'Whodunit'!

In another police force not too far away, it just so happened that another chief constable was having PC/typing error problems also, with regards to revelations about his apparent past.

The *Police Guardian* newspaper-cum-magazine, distributed around the police service, reported his appointment as thus: 'In 1976, he was selected for the Special Course for Young Offenders . . .'

What it should have read was the 'Special Course for Young Officers'.

Don't think he was too pleased with them.

Frankie the Flop

● ● ●

One of my biggest problems when managing and performing with the Scottish folk band was Frankie!

Frankie was like the proverbial 'dug on heat'.

He was desperate – if he was a woman he would have been referred to as a strumpet, his behaviour was that of an out-and-out slapper who you couldn't trust to leave in the same room for two minutes with your granny!

I know this from experience, having observed him over several months, and saw him lumber some of the weirdest-looking humans, for want of a better description, and take them home.

It's frightening to think how these people felt when they woke in the morning and turned around to see Frankie lying in the bed beside them! Aarghhh!

Anyways, the story is, we were touring Moscow and I specifically made the decision that no females would travel back to our hotel in the band's tour bus after a concert.

That said, Frankie, outwith my hearing, decided to organise another form of transport for two girls.

Back at the hotel, Frankie shared a twin room with me and I totally refused to allow him to bring them anywhere near my room.

As a result, he offered another band member $30 to let him use his room.

A further $10 were spent on his condoms.

In the meantime, I was sitting in my room having a few whiskies with our Russian tour agent Vitaly and a couple of the other band members, when out of the blue Vitaly said, in a rather matter-of-fact tone of voice, 'A toast! To Frankie, for tomorrow, he will be dead!'

I raised my glass to my mouth, then realised what he had just said.

'What do you mean, he will be dead?' I asked.

'Unless he pays the small girl for having sex with the tall girl, he will be dead. They work for Russian Mafia!'

I immediately put down my glass and ran out the room to the elevator, got off at the floor where he had taken them and knocked on the room door, ignoring the 'Do Not Disturb' sign.

A few moments later, Frankie opened the door wearing only his kilt and with more fake tan stripes down his chest than Tony the Tiger.

'Aw, whit is it now, Harry?' he said, really annoyed at my intrusion. 'I'm in the middle of something which has nothing to do with you, or the band, so what is it?'

As I looked over his shoulder, I could see the smaller girl, sitting fully clothed on a chair with a mobile phone in her hand, and the other girl half naked on the bed.

'I'm sorry, Frankie! But I just thought you should know, those burds work for the . . .' I then spelled out 'M-A-F-I-A'.

Frankie, fake tan and all, turned a whiter shade than Michael Jackson while taking on a worried look.

He gulped and said, 'Oh fuck! Help me, Harry. What will I do?'

'Well, I think first of all I would immediately develop a severe migraine, or better still, I'd tell them I've just informed you about a death in your family,' I suggested.

'Who is it that's deid?' he asked in all seriousness.

'You are!' I replied. 'If you don't get them out of there pronto. And don't be bringing them anywhere near my room . . . Take them as far away from here as possible!'

'Like, take them where?' he asked.

'Siberia would be a good starting point,' I answered.

I then ran back down to my room, where Vitaly was happily helping himself to my malt in my absence.

'Why didn't you tell me about them sooner?' I asked.

'I did. I tried to tell him, but Frankie, he can only think with his penis, so his head was empty,' he replied.

Moments later, there was a knock at my room door and as I opened it, Frankie was standing there, holding his jacket and kilt belt.

'Are they away?' I asked him. 'Tell me they've gone!'

'Well, not exactly,' he said. 'They're standing along at the elevator, waiting for me to pay them to leave!'

'How much do they want paid?' I asked.

'Two hundred dollars!' he blurted out.

On hearing that, I did what any self-respecting, decent living person in my position as the band manager would do.

I told him to fuck right off and slammed the door shut in his face.

Bang, bang, bang! I opened the door again.

'Please, Harry, please just lend me the money and deduct it from my pay for the tour!'

'Why should I?' I said. 'You brought this on yourself!'

''Cause I'll give two-fifty back,' he answered.

I reluctantly agreed and gave him the money to pay them off and be rid of them for good.

Later that night, while finishing off the rest of my whisky, I asked him, 'Did you not suspect there was something not right about them two?'

'Well, looking back now, the wee yin did all the negotiating and told the big yin whit to do, while she sat in a chair and just watched us,' he explained. 'I just thought she was kinky and would join in later.'

'What about the big yin?' I asked. 'Could she not speak any English for herself?'

'Her? She couldn't speak any of anything. She was deaf and dumb!' he replied.

'Well, there's one good thing to come out of it all,' Ian, the lead vocalist said, 'she didn't need to suffer listening to all that shite you spout at us!'

Then Hamish chipped in with some words of wisdom: 'See the next time you feel horny, Frankie? Just have yourself a bit of old rhyming slang, "Frank"! That way, you don't need an agent, you don't need a manager and you can handle yourself. By the way, it's also a helluva lot cheaper!'

A Colourful Life

...

A young punk rocker was arrested for causing a disturbance in a shopping mall and taken to the police station to
be charged.

The elderly cop responsible for processing the prisoners
on the computer summoned the young punk to be brought
before him to note his details.

The punk stood there proudly, with his hair all spiked
and sticking up and dyed with various bright colours –
blue, red, green, orange and yellow. You name a colour, he
had it.

The elderly cop was somewhat surprised by the young
man's appearance and stared at him for a few moments,
whereby the punk reacted and said sarcastically to him,
'What's up with you, auld man? Have you never done
anything wild in your miserable life before?'

The elderly cop just shrugged his shoulders and nodded
his head, before he replied, 'I have, son. I once got that
drunk I had sex with an African parrot. And just for a
brief moment there, I was wondering if you were the result
of that wild night!'

Little Voice
· · ·

Colin Muir used to be a City of Glasgow cop who transferred down south to work, and one day he was standing
outside the scene of a murder.

A young boy approached and enquired what had
happened, so Colin announced in his Glaswegian accent
(Taggart-style), 'There's been a murder!'

To which the wee boy responded, 'You're from Scotland
Yard. I can tell by your voice.'

Don't Call Us, We'll Call You. Maybe!
· · ·

My old mate Donnie Henderson called me up the other
night and said, 'Hi, Harry boy, how the fuck are you?'

'I'm fine, Donnie, but I'm eager to hear your latest scam
that you wish to involve me in,' I replied.

'Not at all, Harry boy, but I'll tell you what it is. I
phoned that bloody Samaritans mob up for wee blether,
that was all. I just wanted to have a chat with somebody, it
wasn't meant to get suggestive, but I thought we were
forming a wee chatline relationship and she liked me. So I
just asked her to describe what she was wearing.'

'You've got to be kidding! What happened?' I asked.

'She called me a dirty old man and slammed the phone
down on me!' he replied rather despondently.

'She slammed the phone down on you? What, like *this*,
Donnie?' I said, replacing the receiver.

Quiet Please!

• • •

Having babysat a young probationer for several months, I decided it was time he took control and dealt with the next incident while I stood back and watched.

Moments later, we received a complaint of a disturbance between neighbours.

We arrived at the address and spoke with the complainer and were informed that the next door neighbour had been drinking and started arguing with her son and threatened to 'kick his arse' if he didn't move away from the close-mouth.

Having heard their side of the story, we went next door to listen to the neighbour's version.

When we entered, there were two couples, all drinking, and they all wanted to talk at the same time.

So as Graeme, the probationer, asked the woman of the house for her version, he was bombarded with four slightly pissed adults shouting different versions of the incident at him.

It was a total rabble of noise, peppered with swearing.

I stood back, waiting for Graeme to take charge, until I could take it no more and shouted at the top of my voice, 'Shut up!'

Unfortunately, I frightened the life out of poor Graeme, who physically jumped up, knocking his hat off!

We Have a Winner

• • •

The community involvement inspector, Maggie McLean, was arranging an away day for the kids of the police officers in her station, and as a matter of professional courtesy she extended the invitation to the local fire station.

On the day of the trip, only two wee boys, whose father was a leading fireman from the fire station, turned up to go.

All the children boarded the bus, bound for sunny Troon in Ayrshire for their away day, with the promise of fun, games and prizes.

Within a very short time they had arrived at Troon, where they immediately set about arranging games and racing competitions for all the children to keep them occupied and, most of all, tire the wee buggers out!

First up was the sack race, where the two sons of the fireman won, coming in first and second place.

Next was the egg and spoon race, where the two sons of the fireman again won, coming in first and second.

This was followed by the three-legged race, duly won by – you've guessed it – the fireman's sons.

Then it was the under-tens fifty-metre dash, and in first place was the youngest of the fireman's sons.

What about the under-twelves sixty-metre dash? In first place was the other son of the fireman.

The races were coming fast and furious, with, surprise, surprise, the fireman's children winning first and second place *every bloody time!*

After the games were all finished and the trophy haul

handed over to the fireman's sons, the entire group went off for a slap-up meal, with all their favourites on the menu: burgers, pizza, chips with curry sauce, ice cream, chocolate fudge; you name it, they ate it.

At the end of the trip, they were all starting to board the bus for home and Maggie, the inspector, was doing a head count of all the kids and discovered two of the children were missing.

One of the community cops' children spotted right away that it was the fireman's sons.

The inspector instructed Kevin Cuthbert, one of the police officers assisting, to go and look for them.

As he entered the toilets, there they both were, trying to see who could pee the highest up the wall.

Kevin was angry and told them to finish off doing the toilet and get out to the bus, where everyone was waiting.

He then went outside and informed Maggie that he had found them and told her what they were doing.

'What did you do?' Maggie asked him.

'Well, I hit the roof!' Kevin replied.

To which Maggie heaved a sigh of relief and said, 'Thank goodness we've won some bloody thing today!'

A Fond Memory

· · ·

I joined the City of Glasgow police about the same time as an Irish boy called Harry MacAleer.

Harry, was very good at playing the great Highland bagpipes and over the next few years, while working out of the Gorbals police station, he would maintain his high standard of piping by practising regularly in the yard during his refreshment breaks.

This was considered acceptable by the subdivisional officer, who was keen on the music, being from Uist.

However, the sound of pipe music and that of police work were about to clash, when a detective officer working in an office immediately above Harry's favourite piping spot was interviewing a suspect on tape.

He had gone through the preamble of the operation with the suspect and was about to ask his first question, when the unmistakeable strains of 'Mull of Kintyre' punctured his eardrums.

As a result of this, the retyped transcript of the interview read as follows:

It is alleged that you are one of the— The time is now 19:52 hours and this interview is now being terminated, because, as you can hear, Harry MacAleer is playing his bloody musical octopus right under the fuckin' Taped Interview Room of the station!

The Glesca Kiss

· · ·

From *The Adventures of Harry the Polis*

(Harry and Spook are working in the front of the police office, talking about the boxing match from the previous night.)

SPOOK: Did ya see Mo-Mo McCulloch boxing last night on da telly?

HARRY: That wasn't boxing. In boxing, you're supposed to use your fists!

SPOOK: And what did ya think he used then?

HARRY: His head, that's what he used!

SPOOK: Away, man, da guy couldn't handle Mo-Mo's left hook, dat's what laid him out.

HARRY: Naw, son! What he couldn't handle was McCulloch's Glesca kiss!

SPOOK: Well, how comes they took him to da hospital afterwards?

HARRY: They didn't! They took him to a hairdresser's to have his mouth washed out with Head and Shoulders shampoo.

SPOOK: Why did they do dat then?

HARRY: Because his mouth was full up with dandruff!

Kleptomaniac, Now That's the Word
· · ·
A woman was arrested for the umpteenth time for shoplifting and taken in by the Central Shoplifting Squad, where she was charged and processed for the court.

The detective asked her, as a regular offender, why she was compelled to persistently shoplift.

The accused replied, 'To tell you the truth, I don't really know, but I think I must be a nymphomaniac.'

To which the detective joked, 'Unfortunately for you, hen, that's a completely different thing and something of an active sport, but you might want to consider taking it up on your release!'

Gordon Bloody Ramsay
· · ·
I received a call one night from a flustered woman motorist, who said she had just hit a pheasant on the Blantyre Farm road.

I confirmed that no one else was injured, her car wasn't damaged and was still driveable.

After I had noted all the relevant details I was required to ask her about, I informed her there was no need for a report.

Still upset by the incident, the lady driver asked me, 'What should I do with the pheasant now?'

To which I couldn't resist replying, 'Well, if you like, I could give you a right good recipe!'

Ode tae Harry the Polis

• • •

Look out! Look about! He's walking his beat
The funniest cop ye're ever likely to meet
He'll move ye alang, he'll even tell ye aff
And fit ye wi' handcuffs, jist for a laugh
Enforcing the law with his extra long arm
Arresting you with his likeable charm
And suddenly you'll realise this is no rumour
The offences regarding his hilarious humour
There's no way to resist it, not even for you
Harry the Polis, Even the Lies are True!
He's totally unbiased, whether Billy or a Dan
Treating all equal, whether woman or man
Ye'll never escape him, for he has his spies
Harry the Polis, and Even More Lies!
Patrolling the area, in his blue panda car
Neds who commit crimes won't get very far
So when ye're arrested, jist zip up yer mooth
Harry the Polis, Nuthin' Like the Truth
He'll tell you a joke, an anecdote, or a tale
Stories full of laughter to keep you out of jail
A bellyful of fun times, with a uniform to fit
Harry the Polis, Ye're Never Gonnae Believe it!
So heed this warning and remember to behave
For the polis are loyal, they're honest and brave
So remain law-abiding and you'll soon see the light
Harry the Polis, Aye, That Will Be Right!
And if you always behave, ye'll stay out of trouble
And no amount of verbals, will burst yer bubble
You'll never appear in court, or utter a porky pie
Harry the Polis, Ah Cannae Tell a Lie!

(The latter is presently under construction.)

Tut, Tut!

. . .

Finally. A police officer was staggering home after a night out with the members of his shift when he saw a chapel door opened and wandered inside and entered a confessional box.

After a few moments there was a sound from the next cubicle like someone clearing their throat.

This was closely followed moments later by the same person making a 'tut, tut' sound.

A short time elapsed, when the person in the next cubicle made another noticeable grunting noise, followed by a louder tut, tut.

Whereupon the drunken police officer said, 'You can 'tut, tut' all night pal, but there's no toilet paper in this cubicle either.'

Harry Says, 'Share With Me!'

. . .

Former police officer Harry Morris, author of the popular *Harry the Polis* series of books, is planning to publish book number six of his funny short polis stories:

Harry the Polis, Ah Cannae Tell a Lie!

He would like to extend an invitation to all serving and retired polis, along with all FSO staff, to contribute a story to future publications and allow the popular, hilarious series to continue.

Stories must be of a humorous nature and can even be a short scenario of an incident that you would like the author to expand upon. (All names will be changed to protect the guilty.)

We are all very much aware of the seriousness and important side of the job, when serving the public. That's why the humour we enjoy in our duties is a very important feature to our work.

So why not share it with your colleagues and the public by giving everyone a laugh, as opposed to reading about horrific day-to-day crimes that we see daily in the press that are forced upon us.

Just send stories, poems, anecdotes, jokes or tales to:

e-mail: harry@harrythepolis.com
web: www.harrythepolis.com

The author will be sure to credit you with your submission. However, if you wish to remain anonymous, this will also be respected by the author. The main objective is not to make fun of the police force, but to write about the humour we all enjoy and contribute to within it.

So why don't you start writing and let me hear from you? We all have a funny story we have been involved with, why not share it?

Thank you

• • •

I hope you enjoyed reading this book of stories in the *Harry the Polis* series as much as I enjoyed writing it.

To all my former colleagues, past, present and future police officers, I would say: if you can't laugh at yourselves, then leave the job to others.